STRESS RELIEVING YOGA RETREAT

&

DISCO FEVER

COLORING BOOK

Stress Relieving
YOGA RETREAT
Yoga Coloring Book

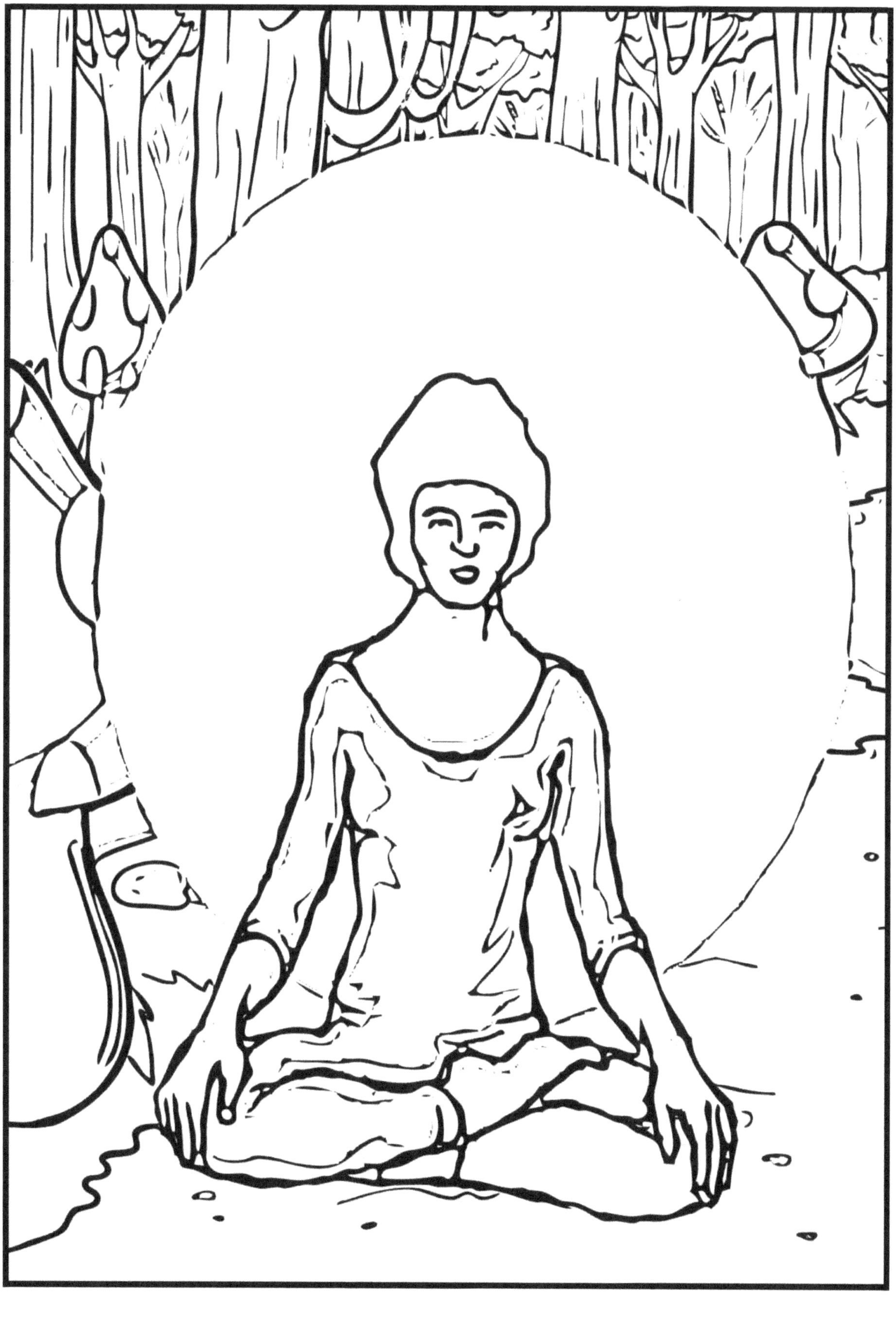

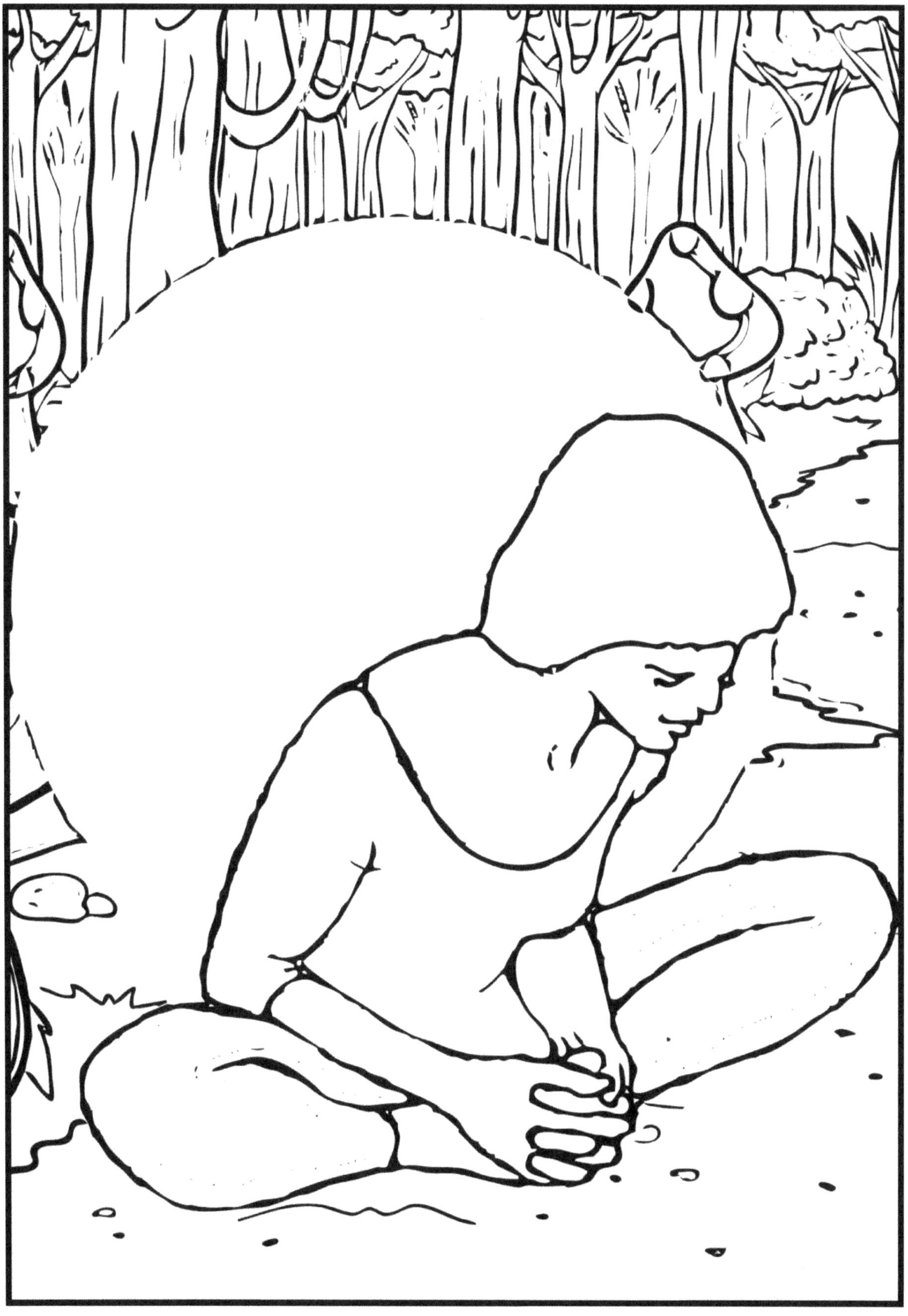

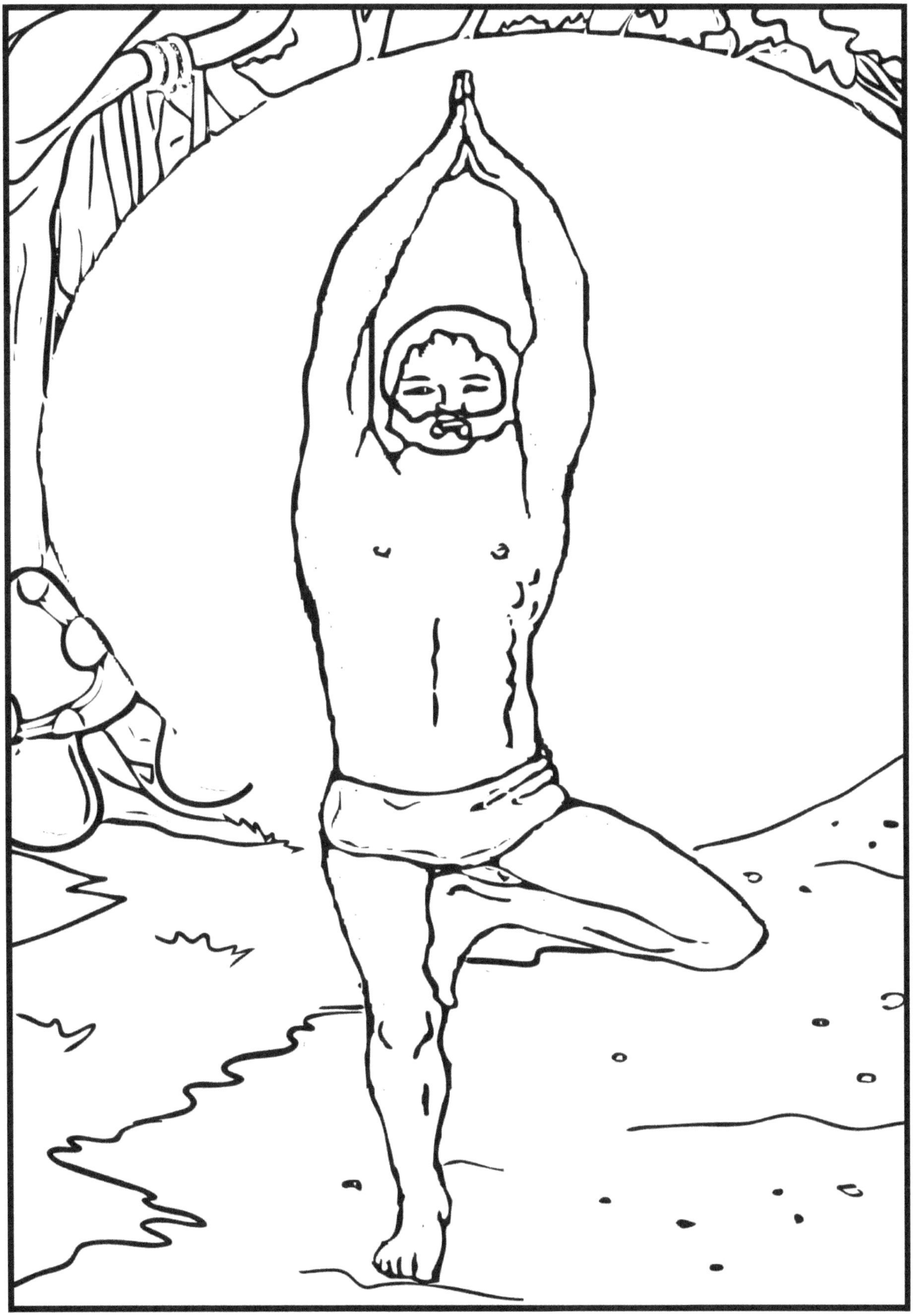

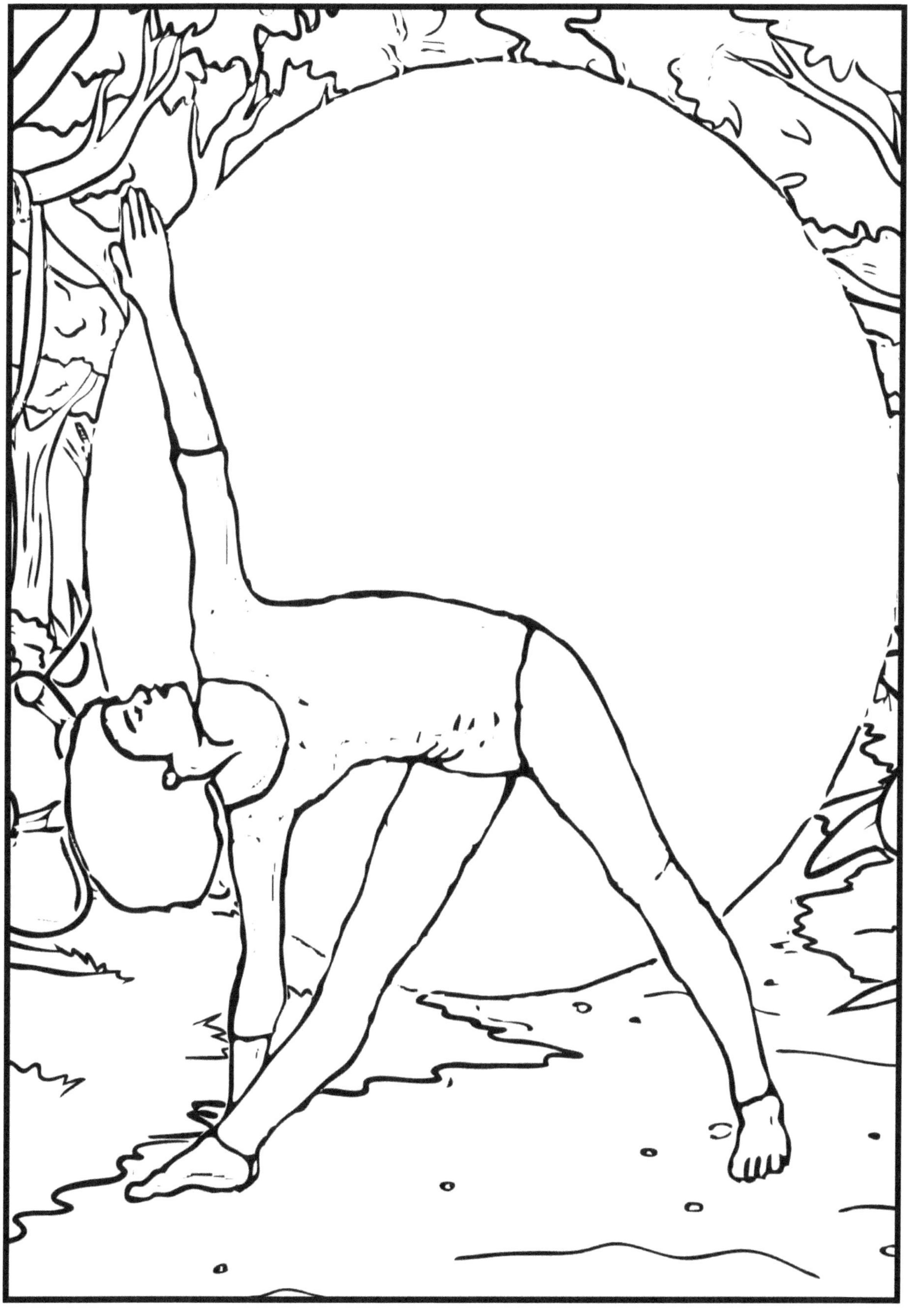

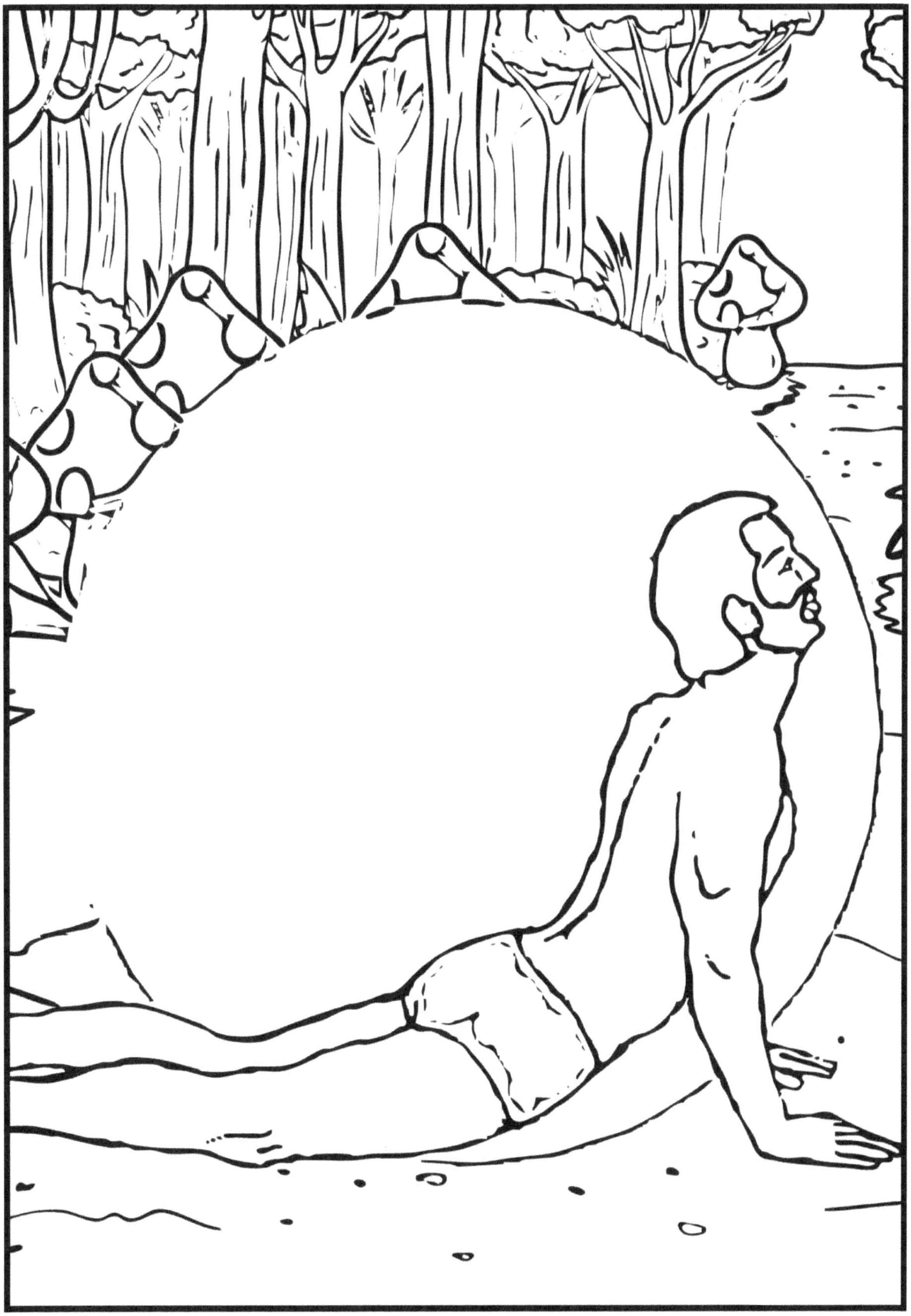

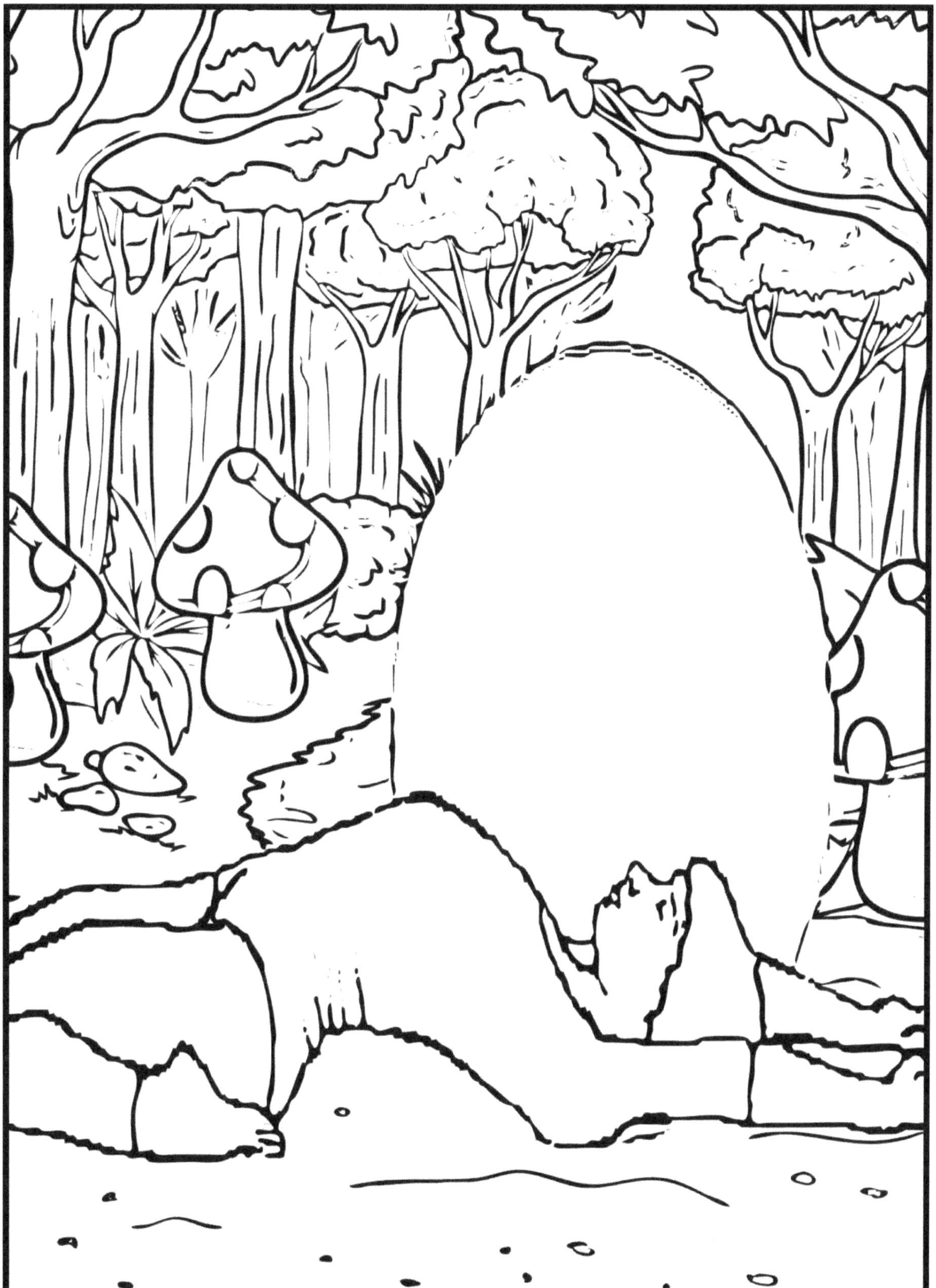

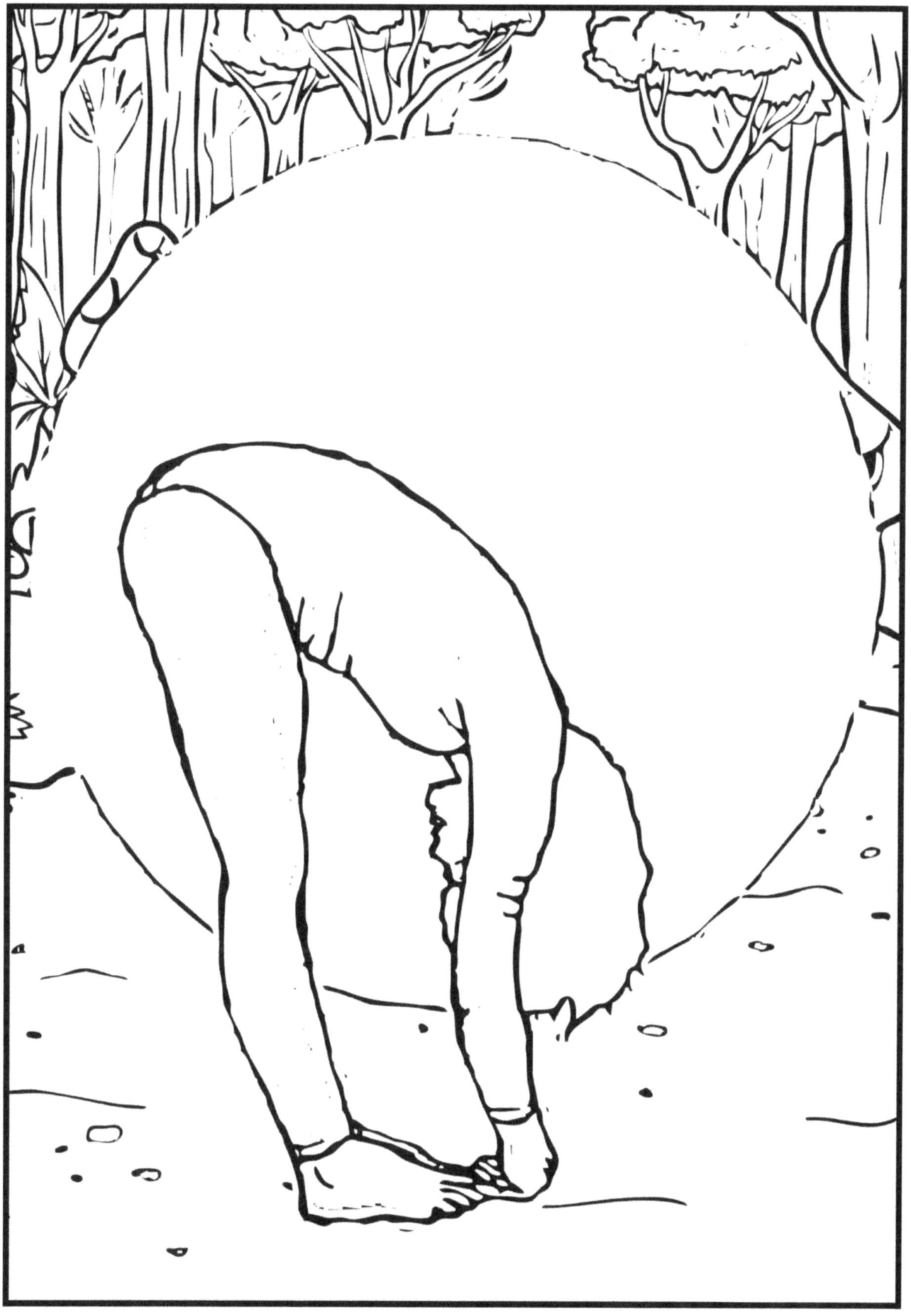

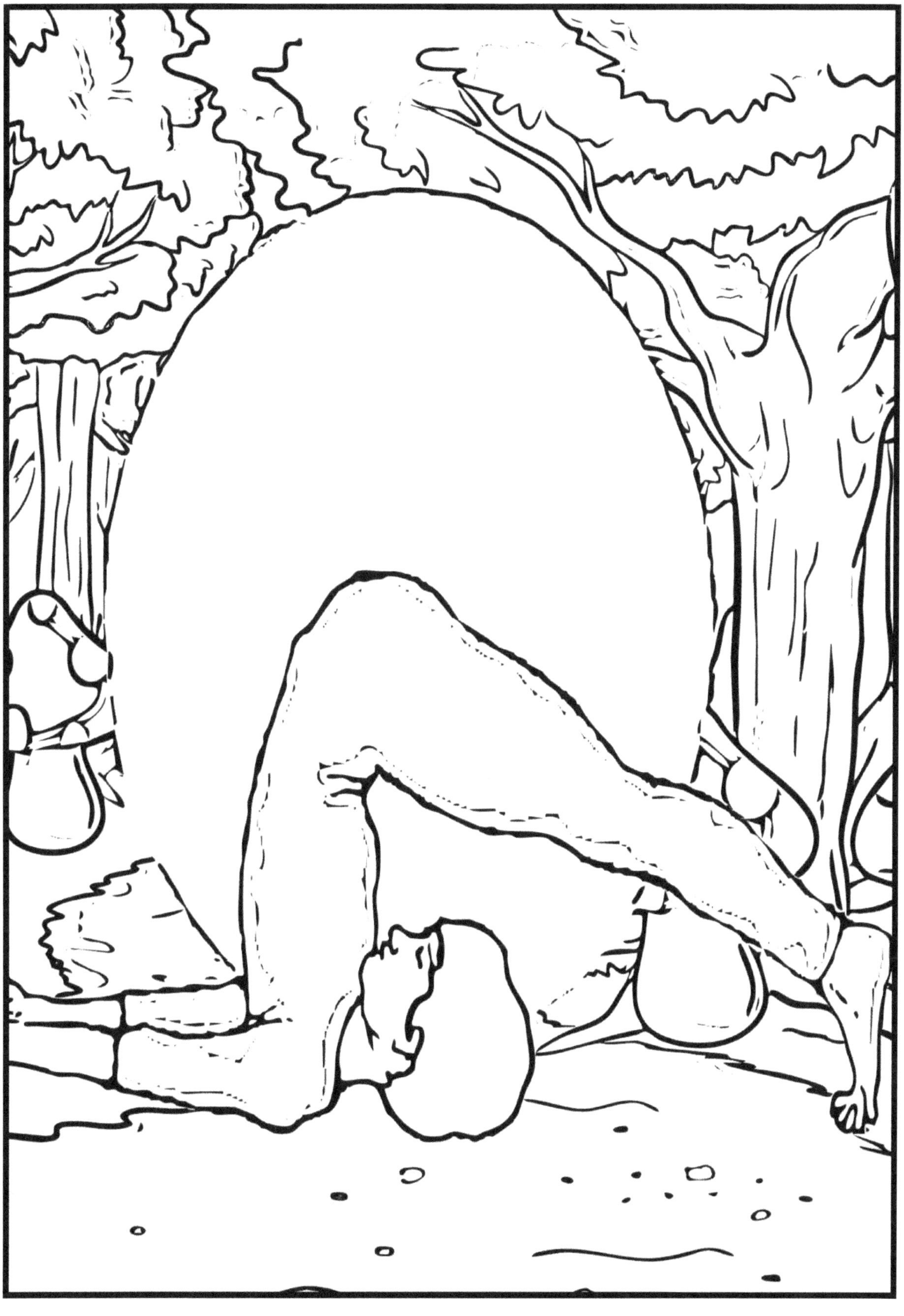

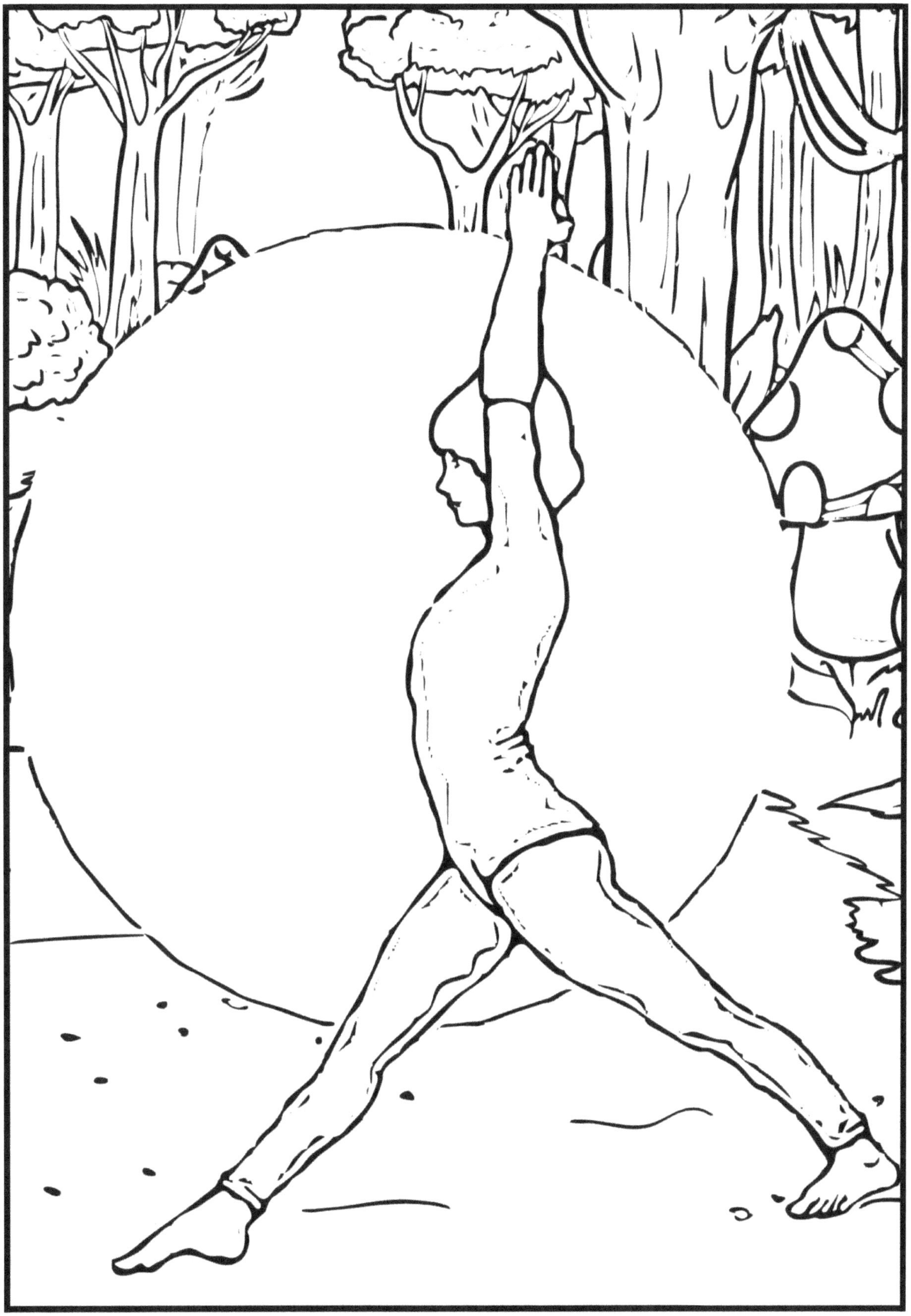

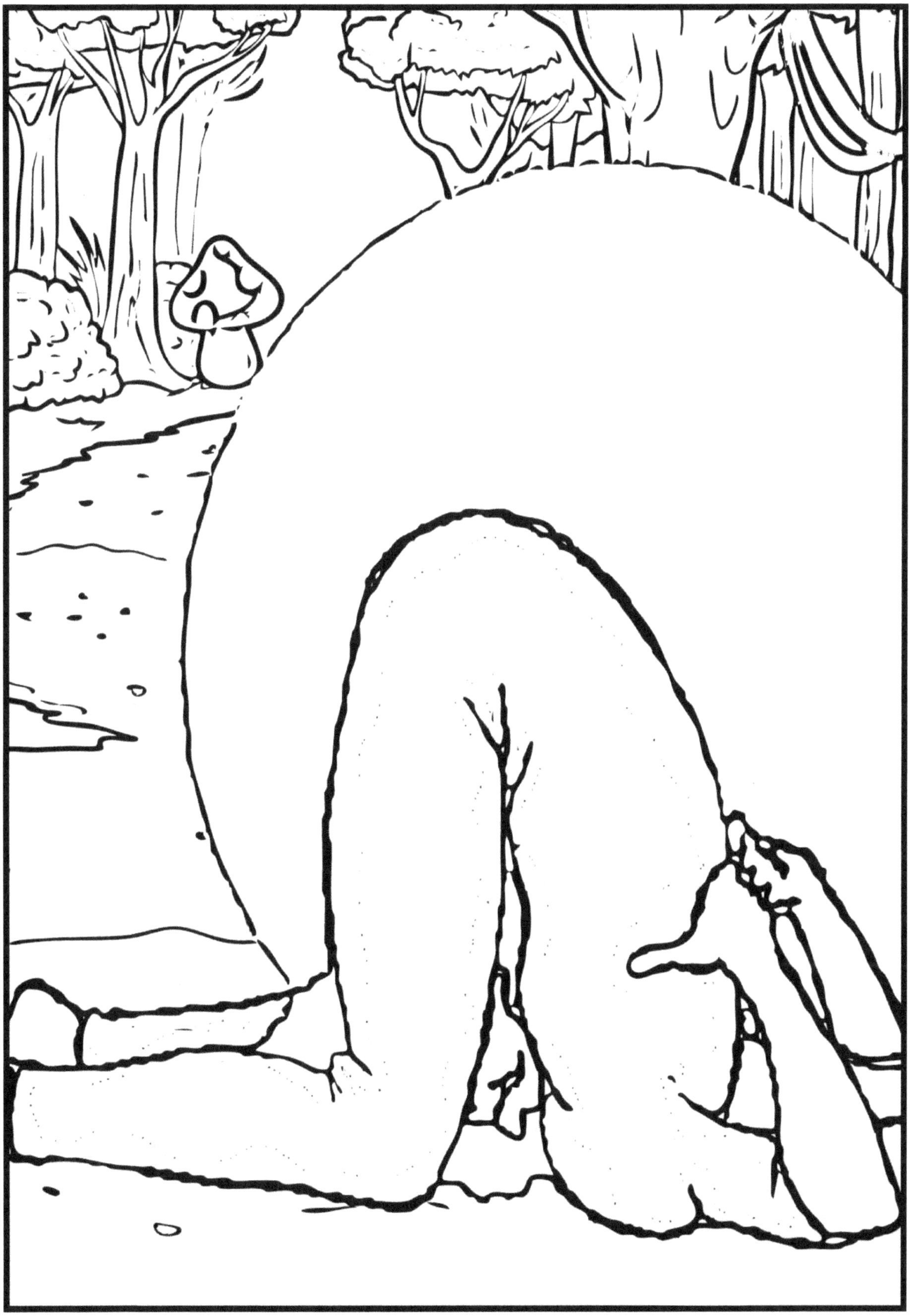

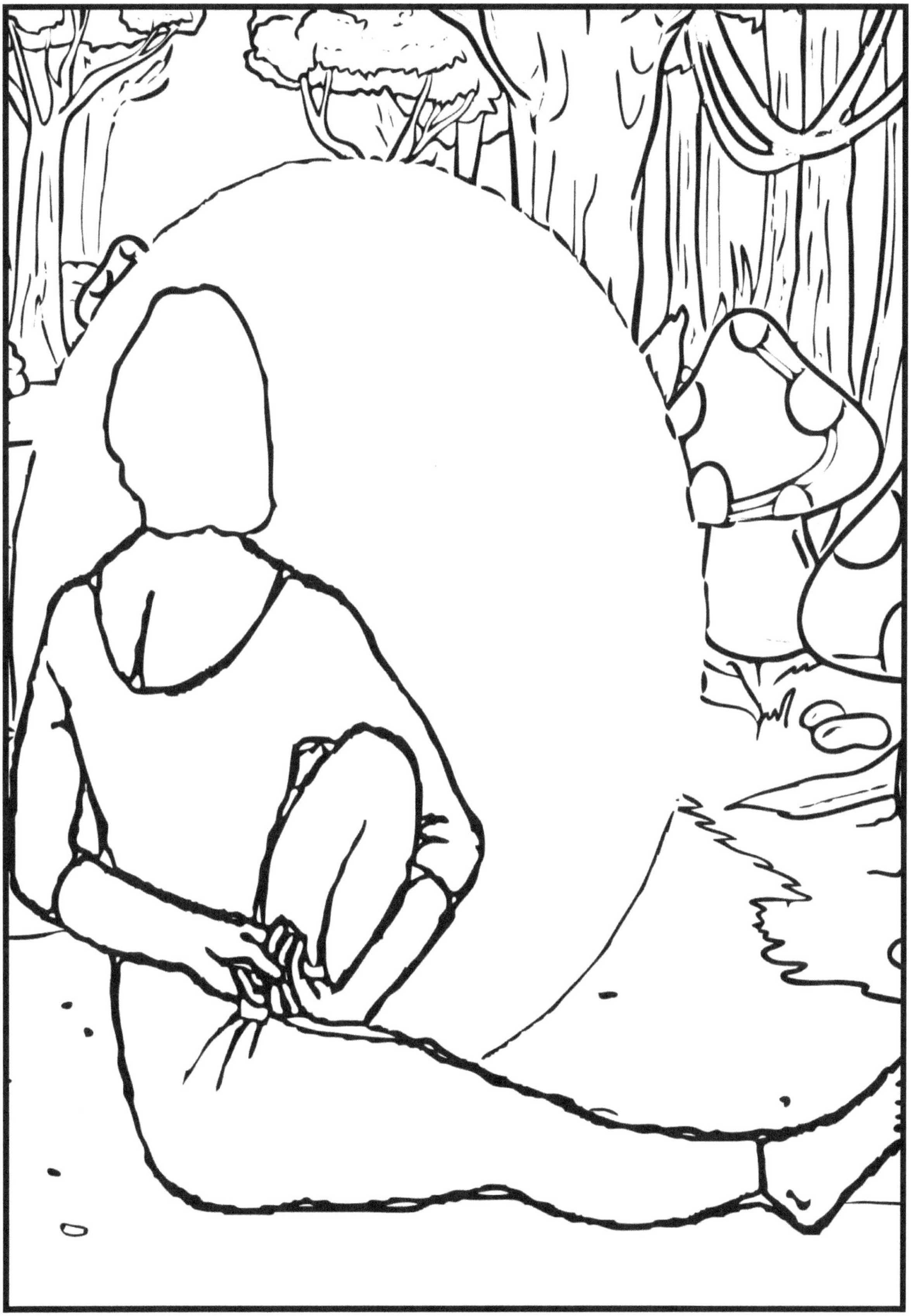

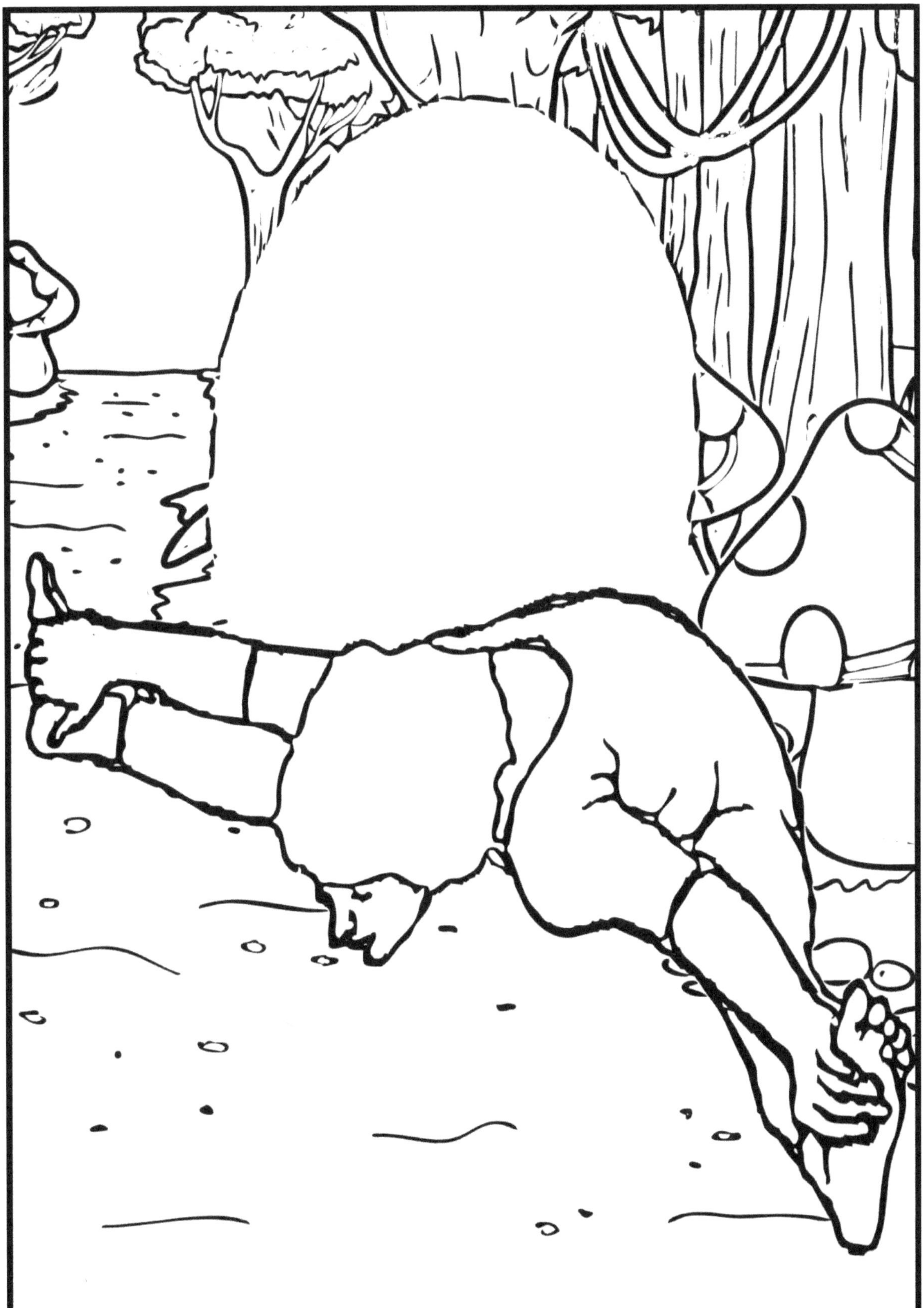

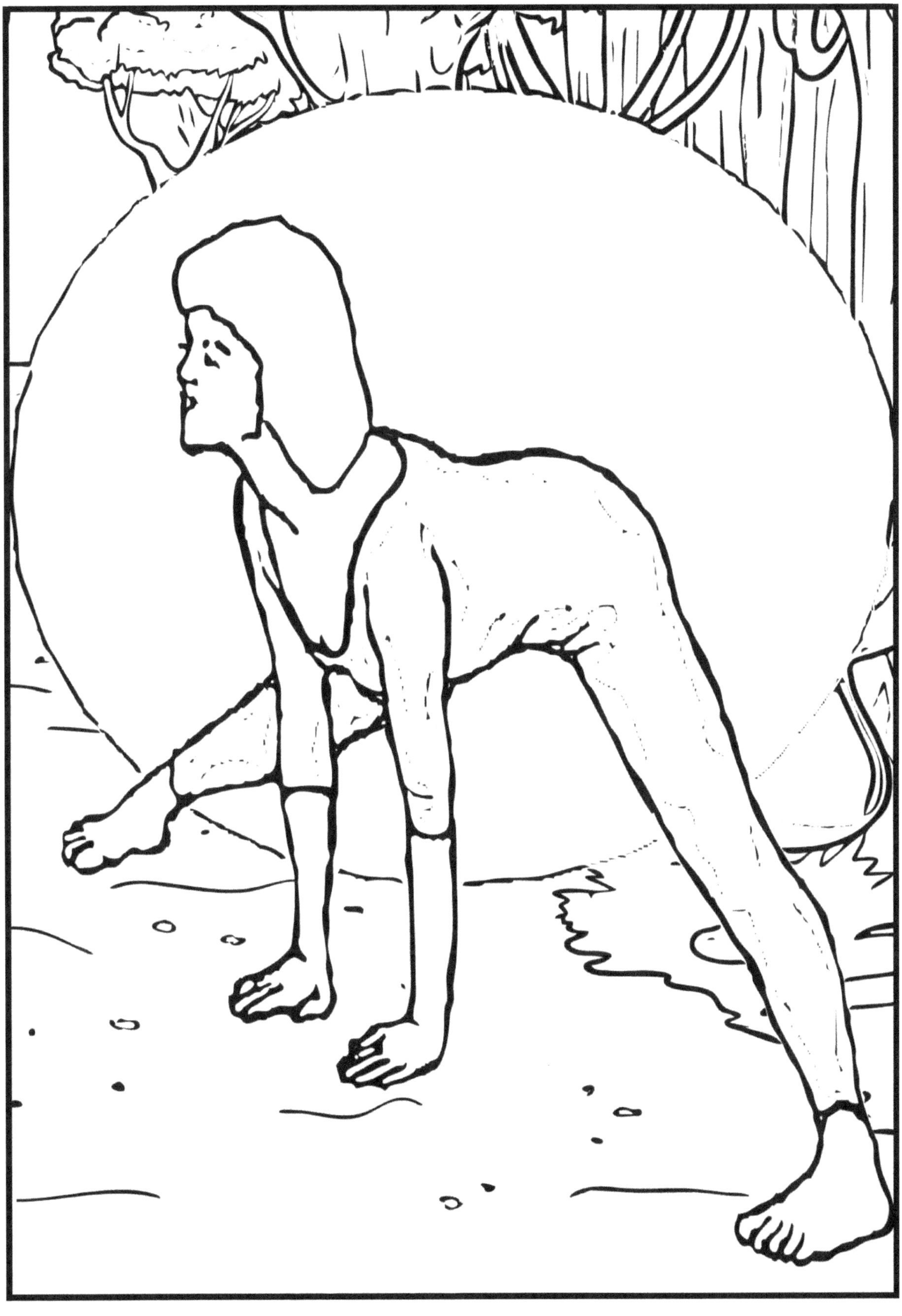

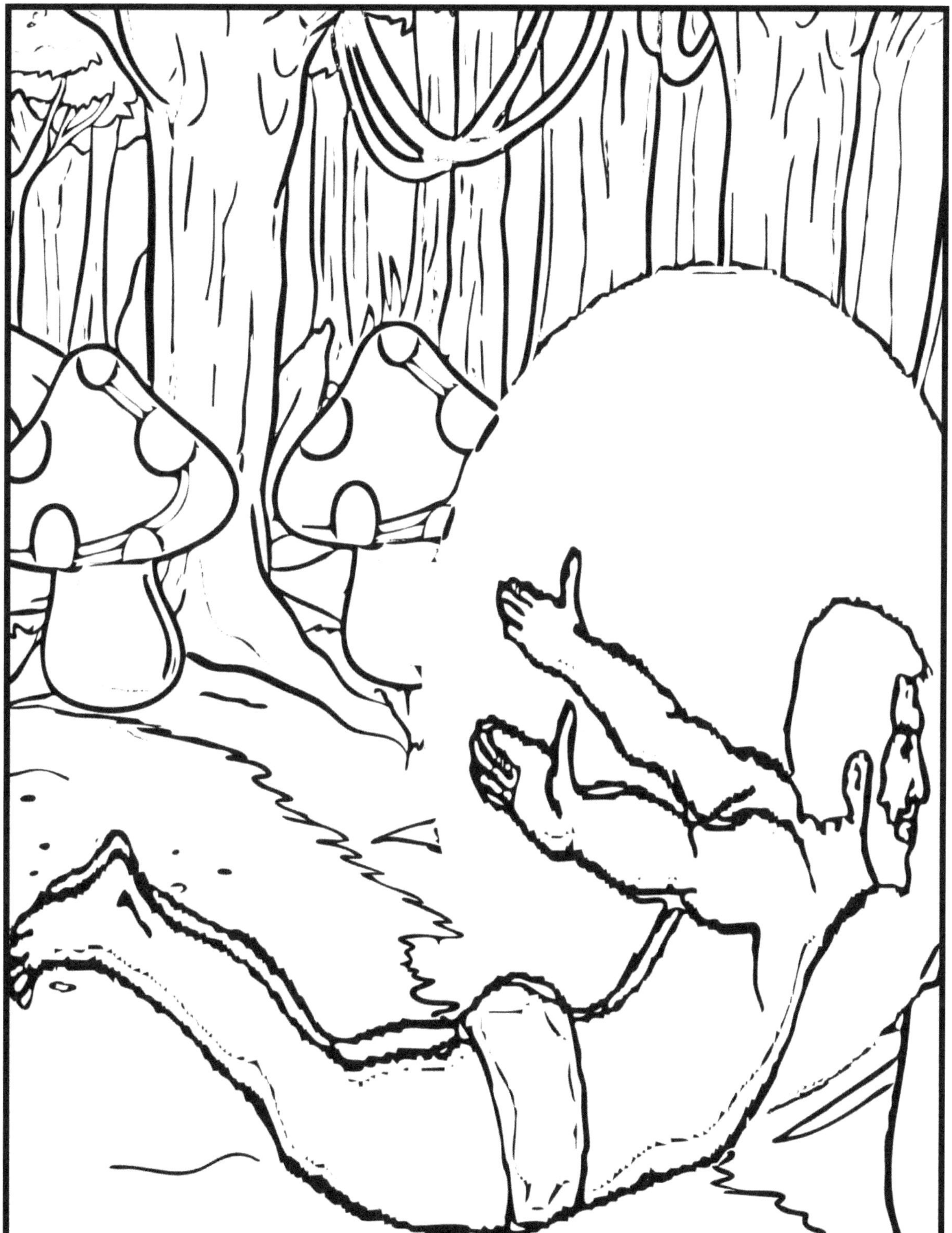

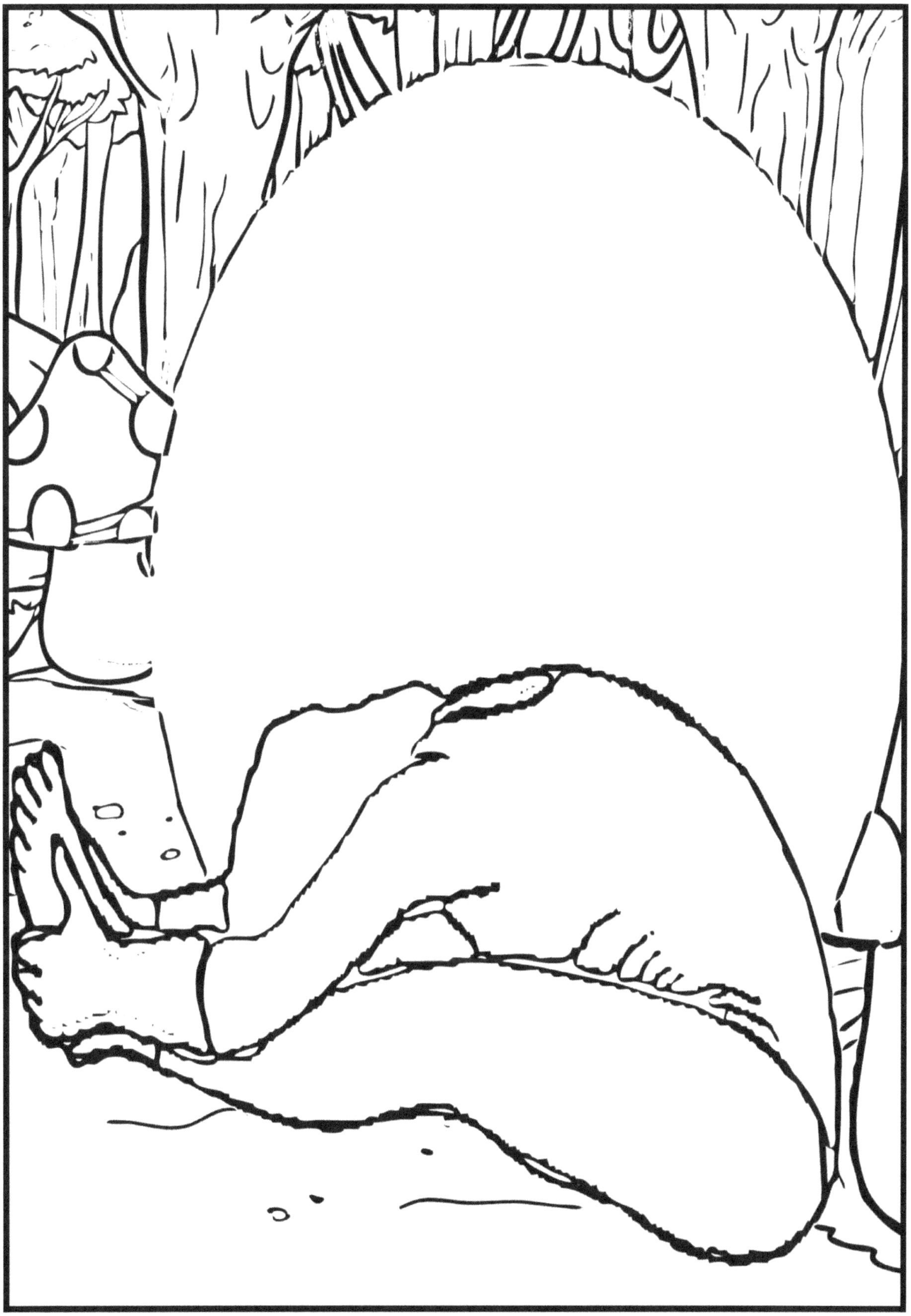

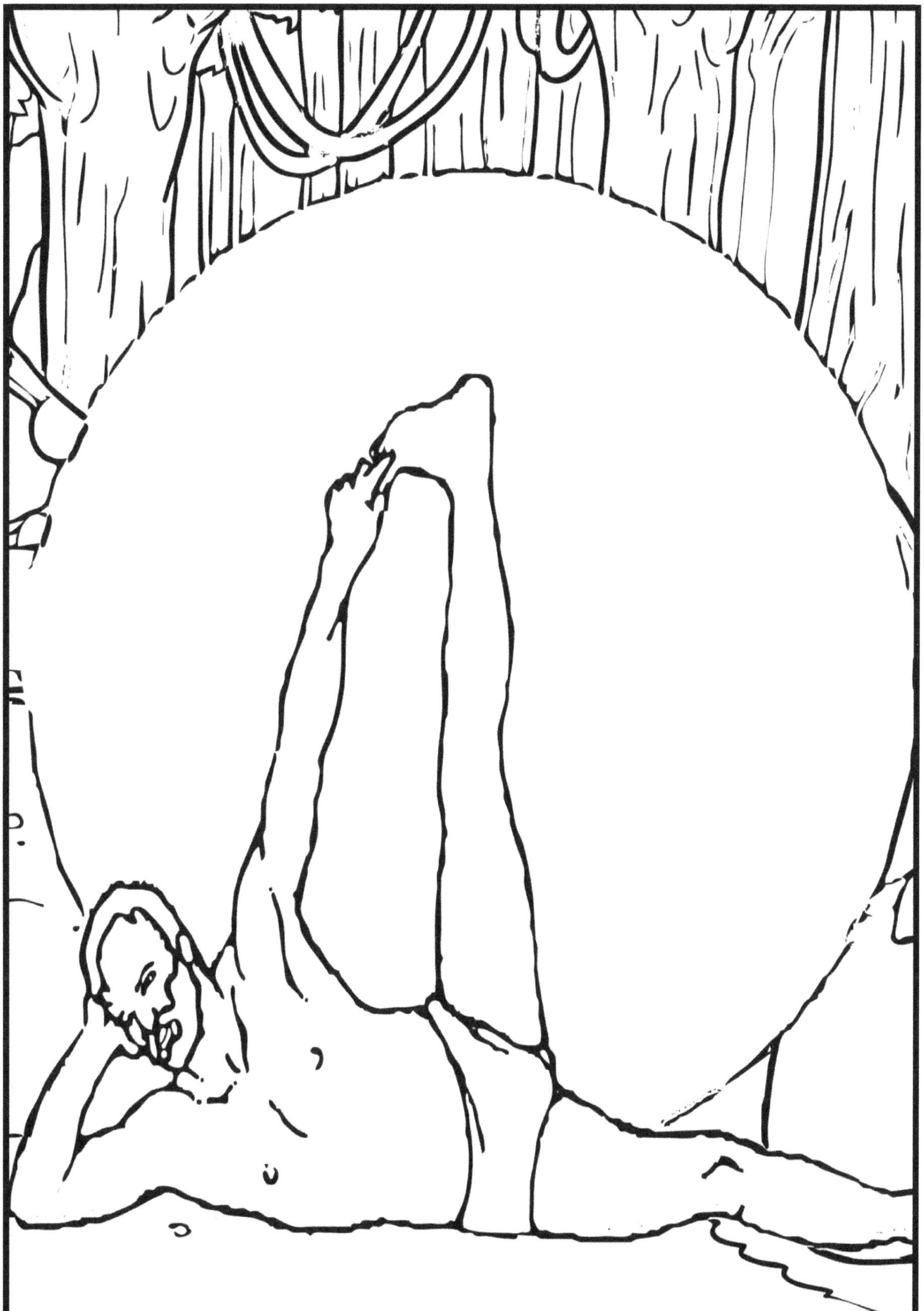

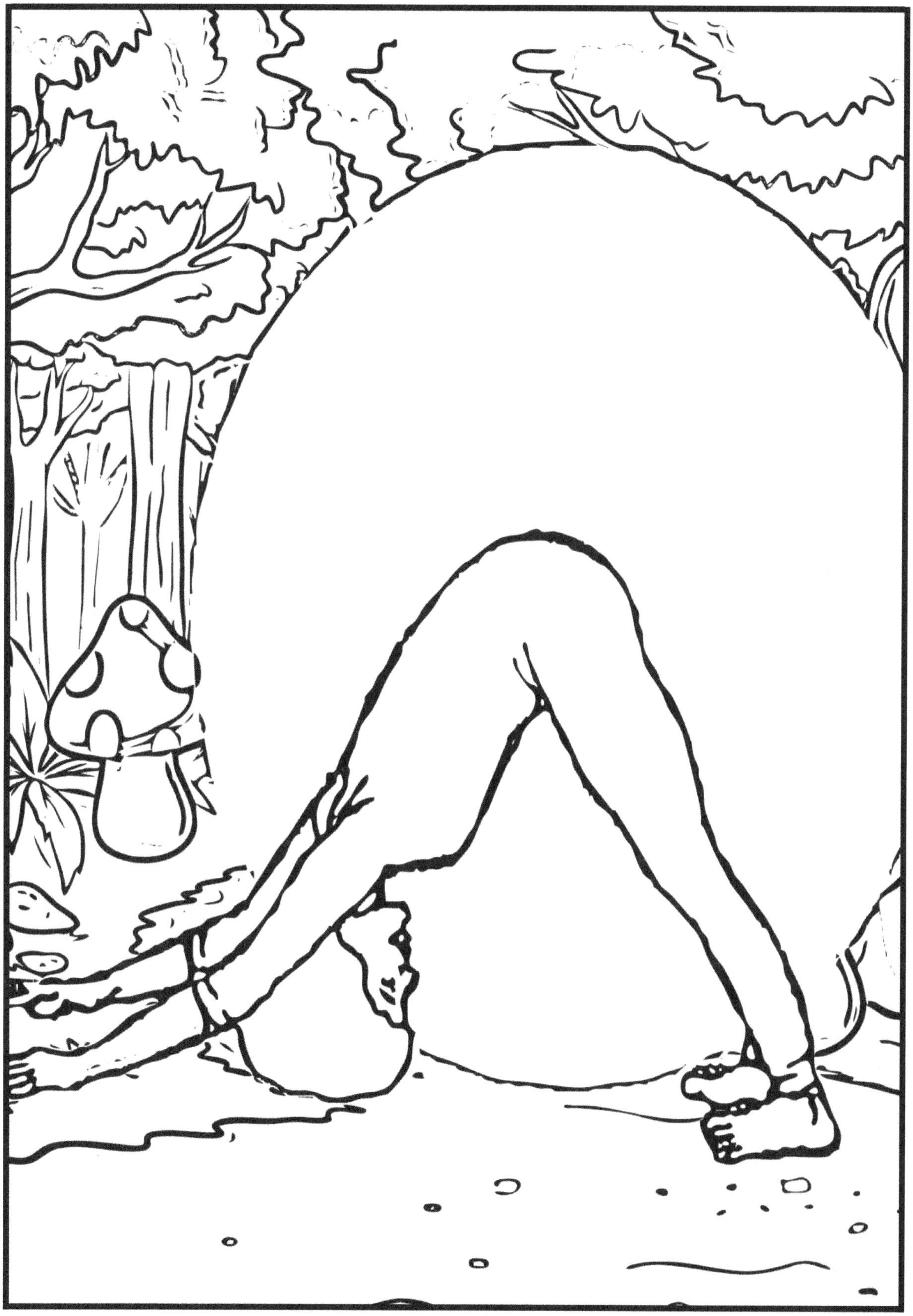

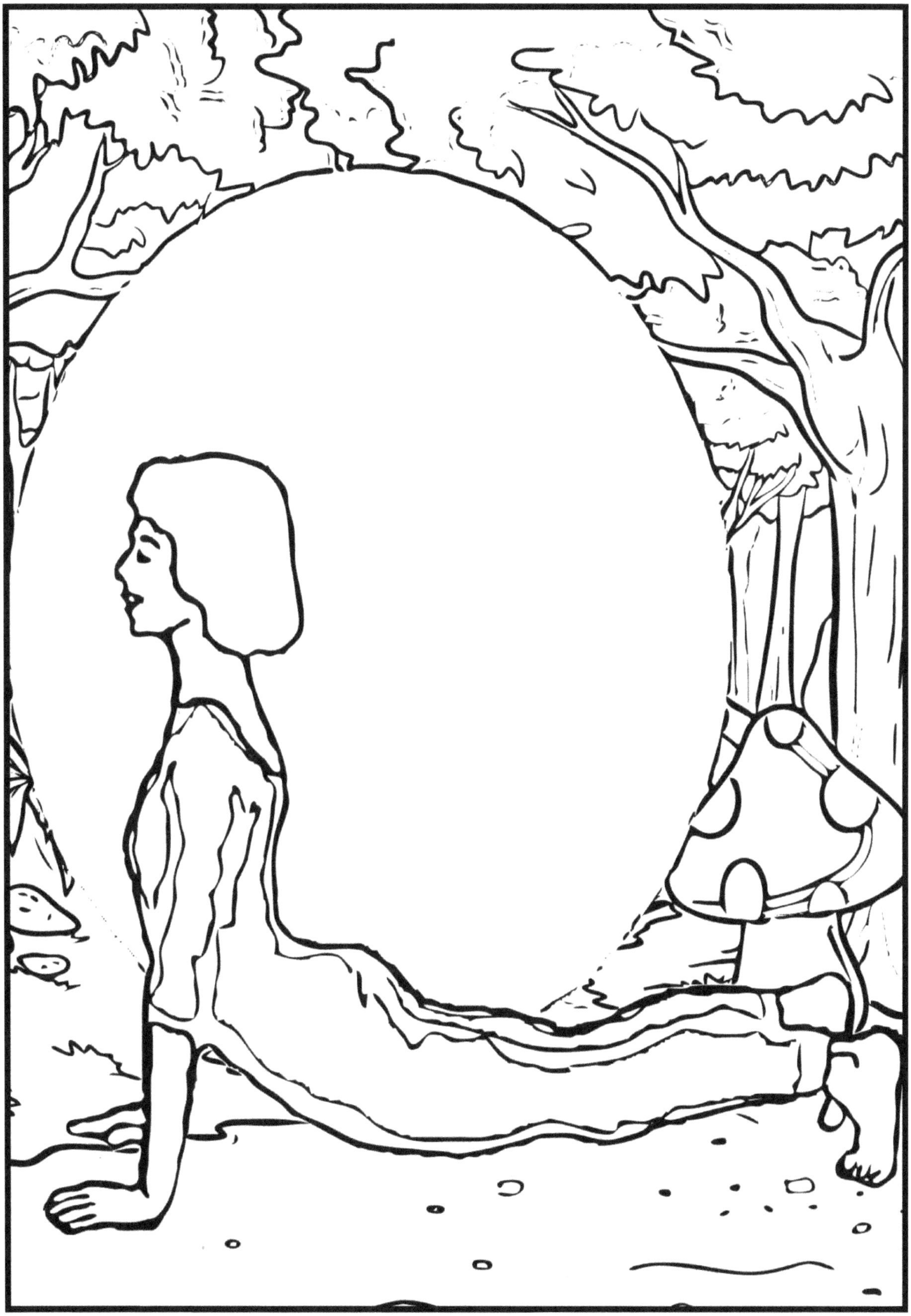

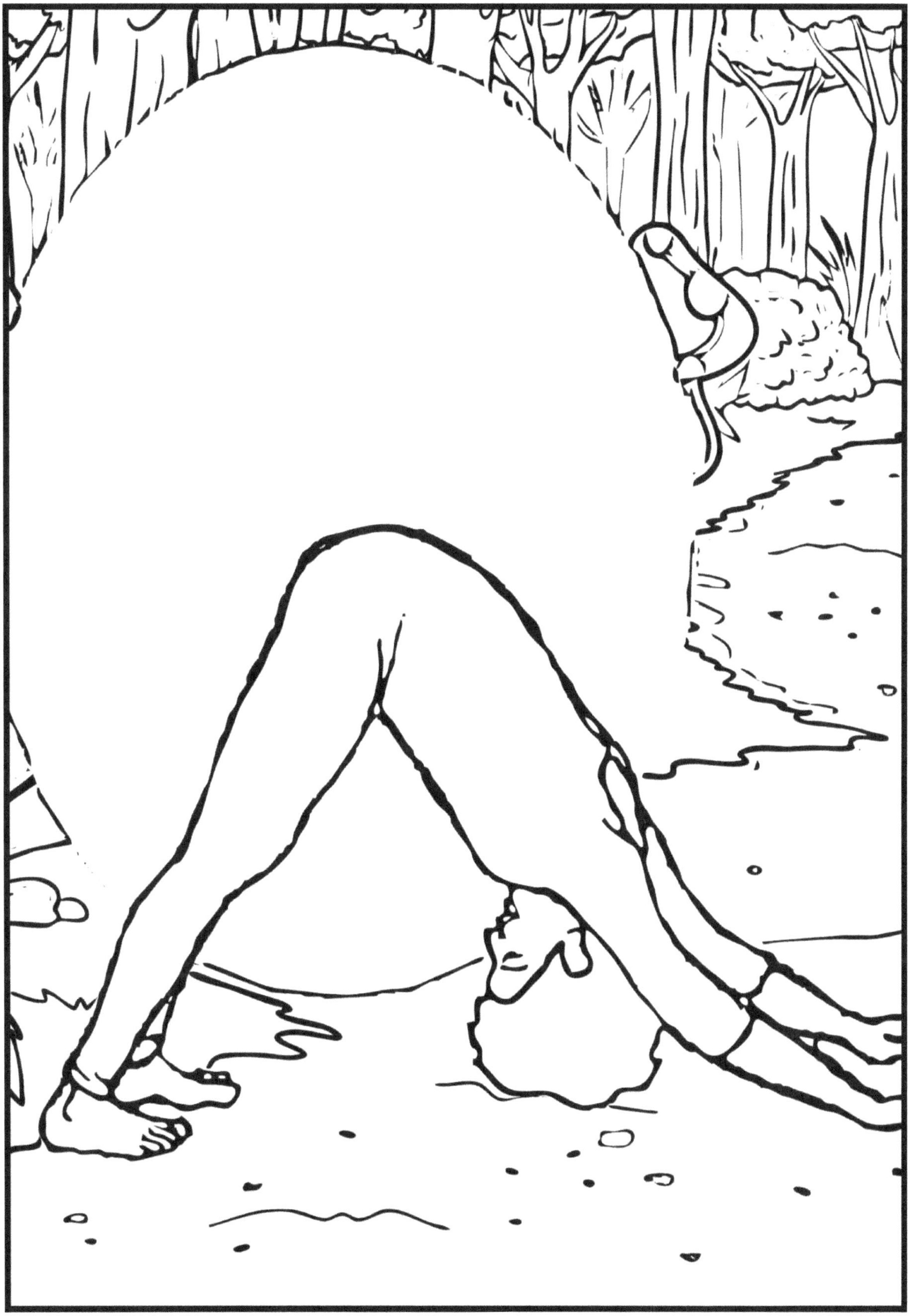

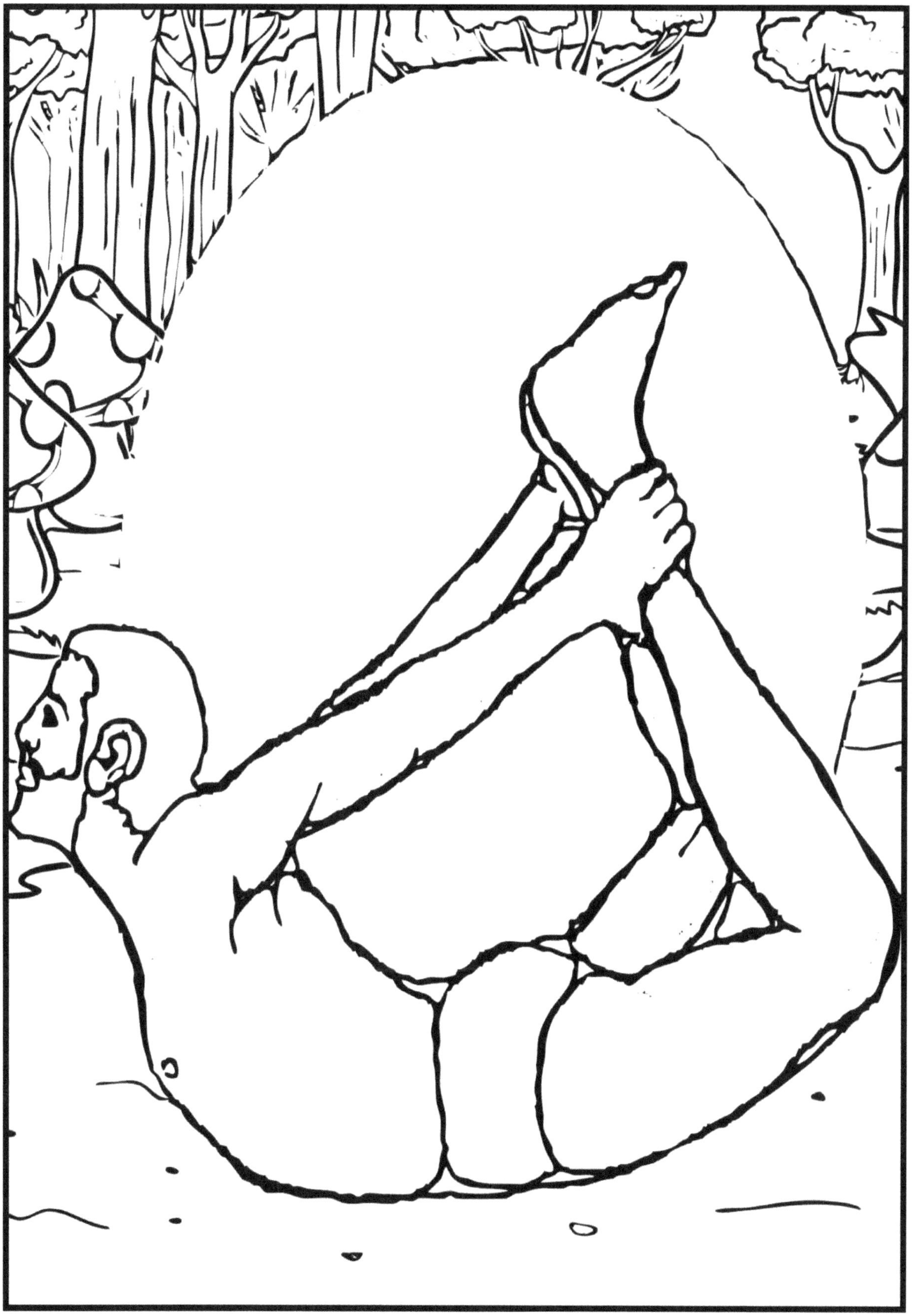

DISCO FEVER
70's Coloring Book

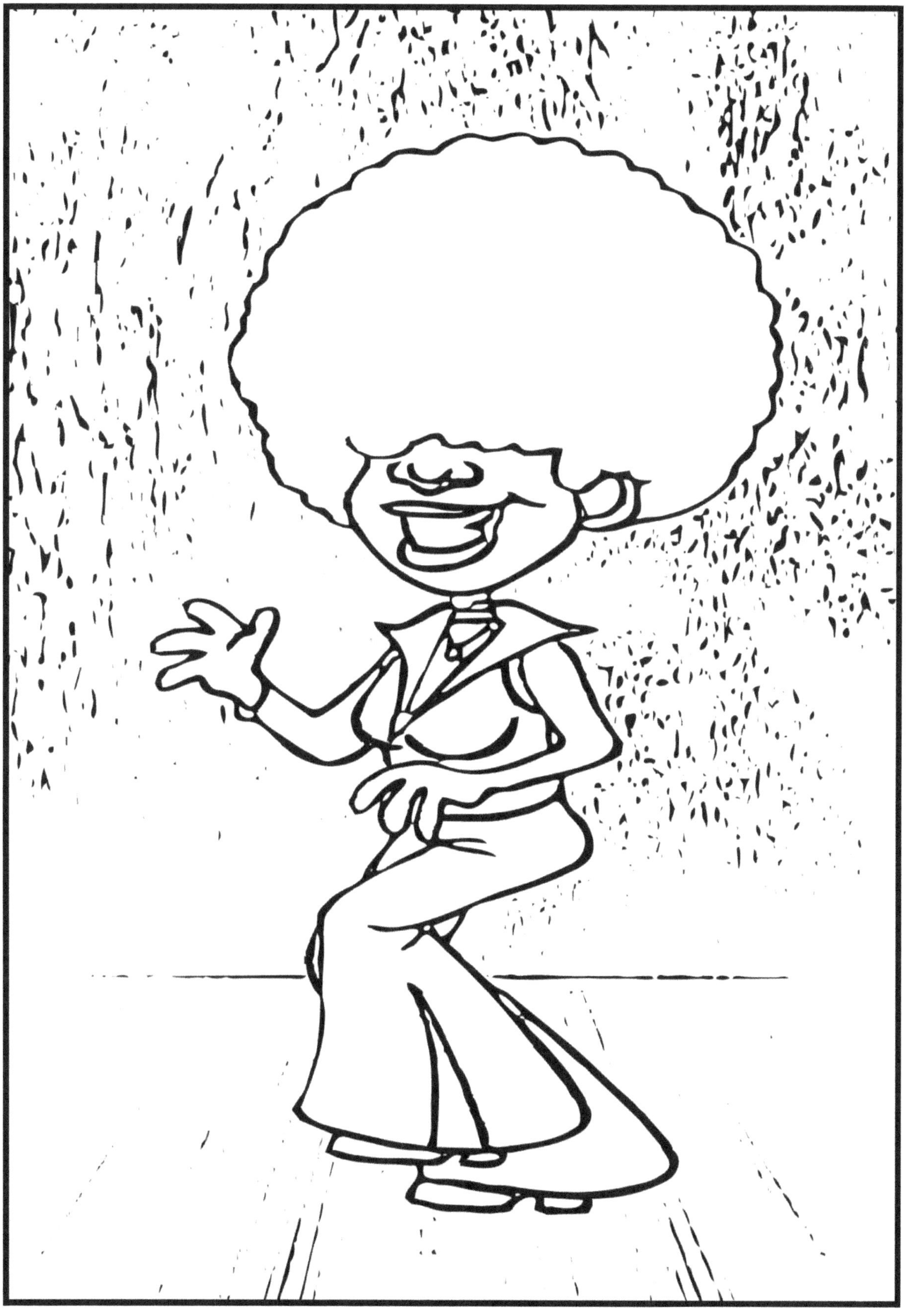

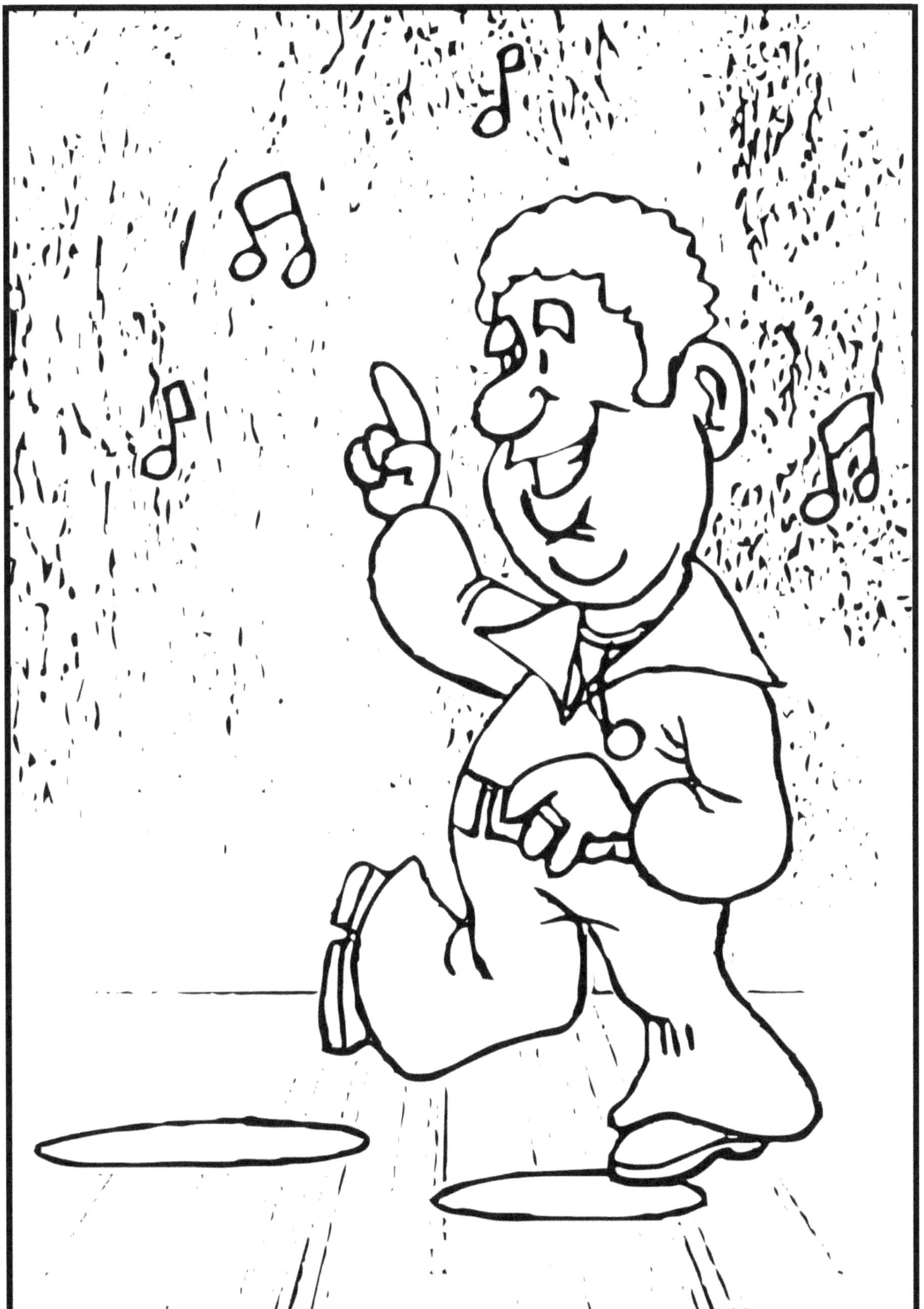

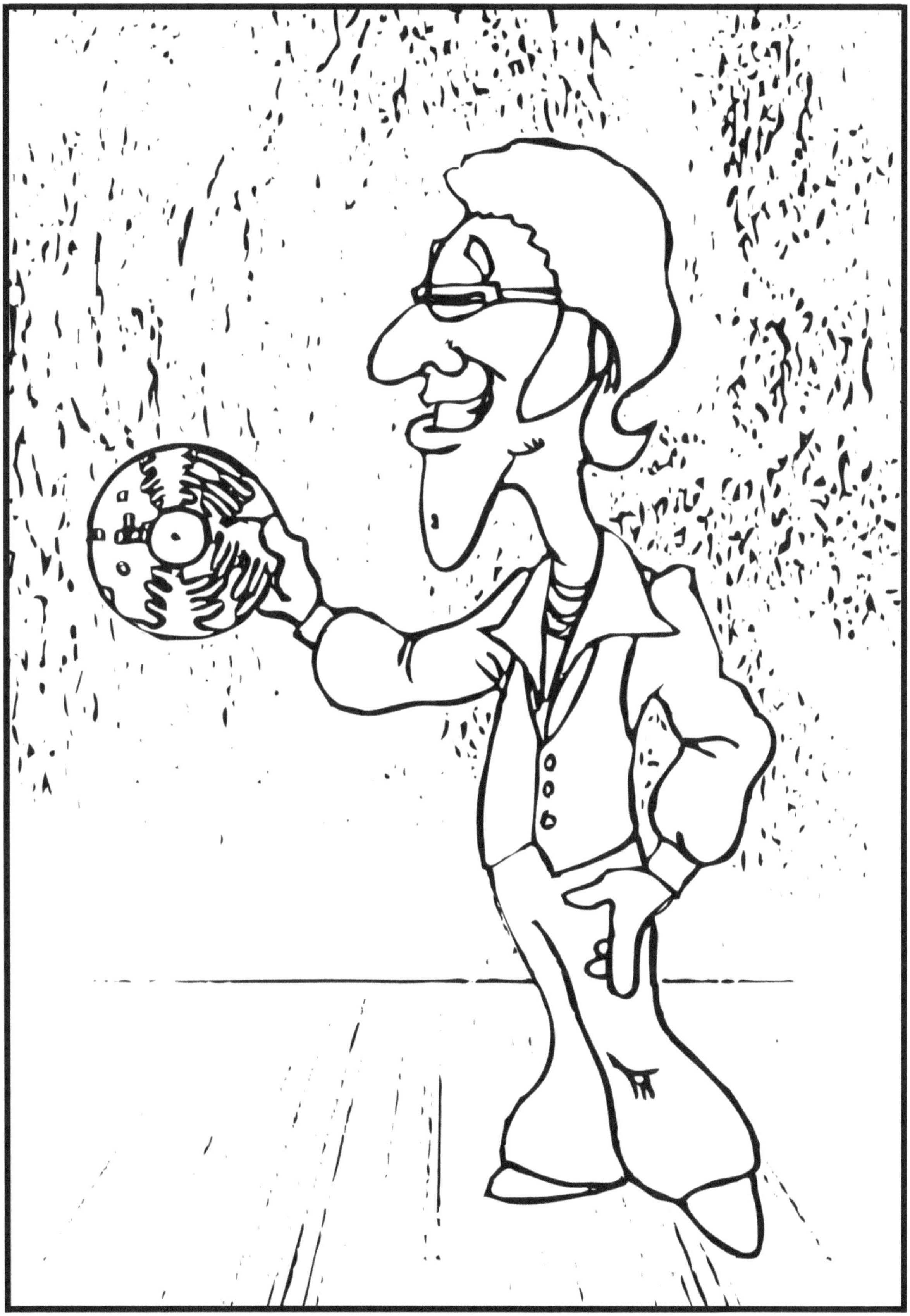

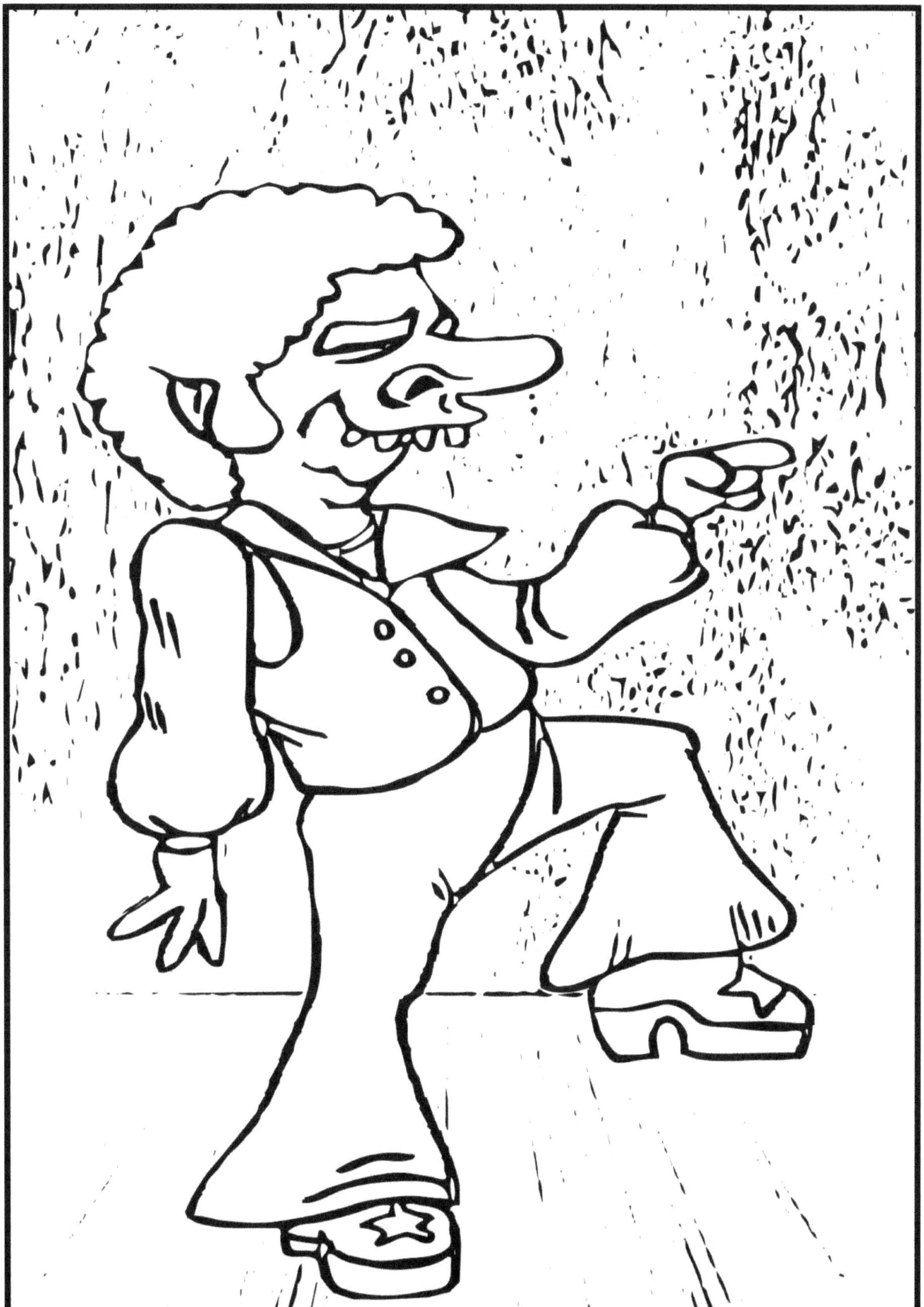

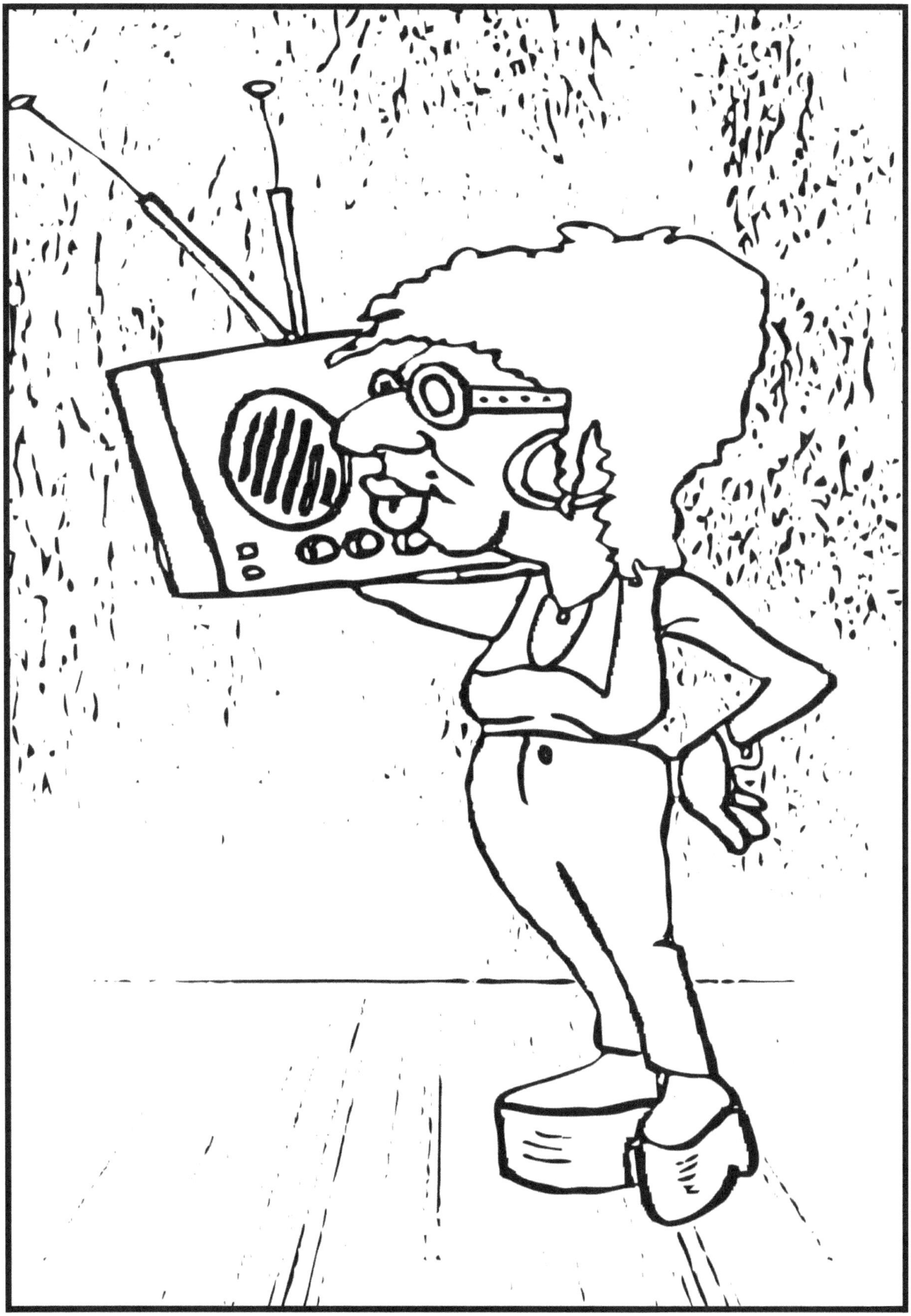

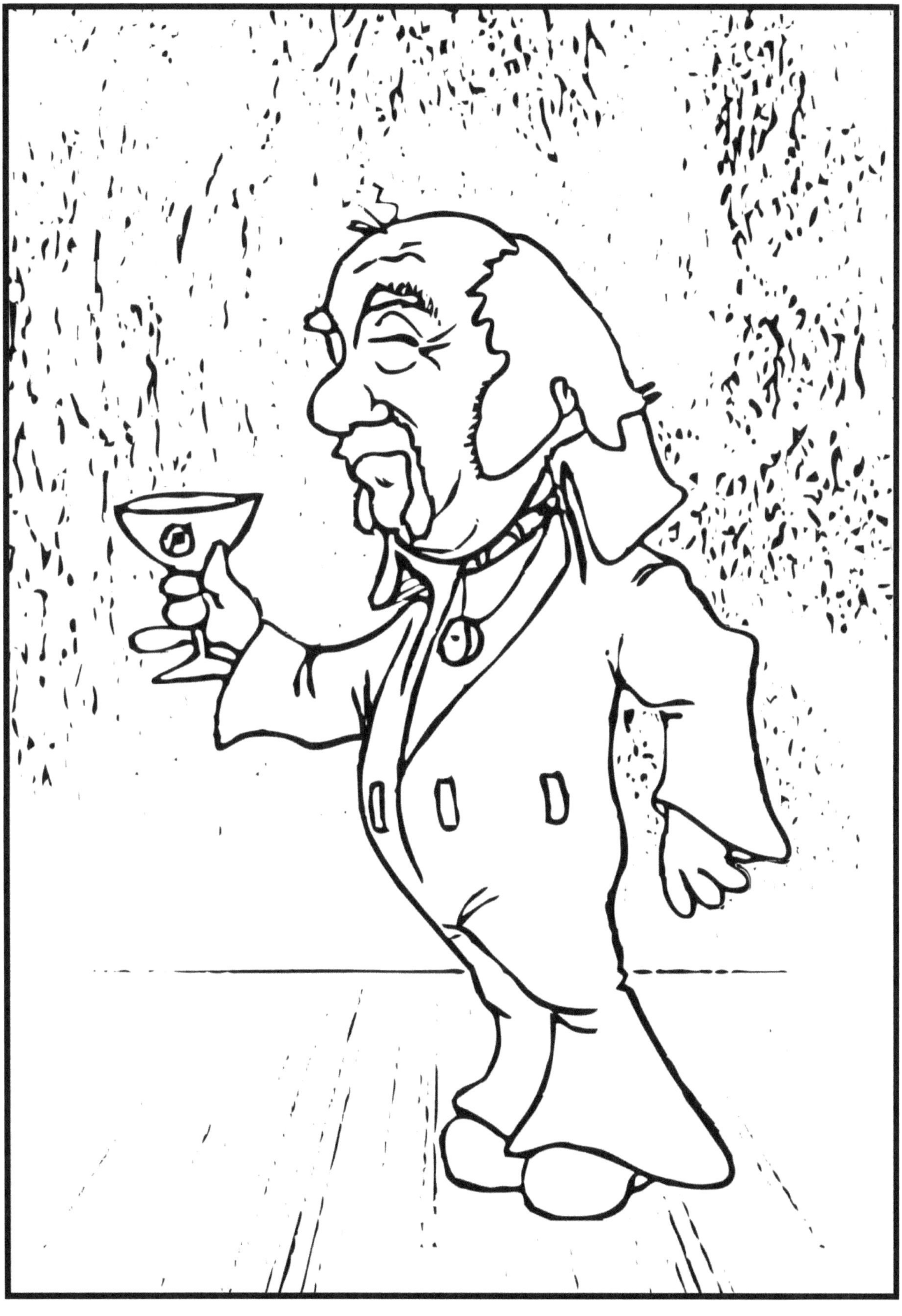

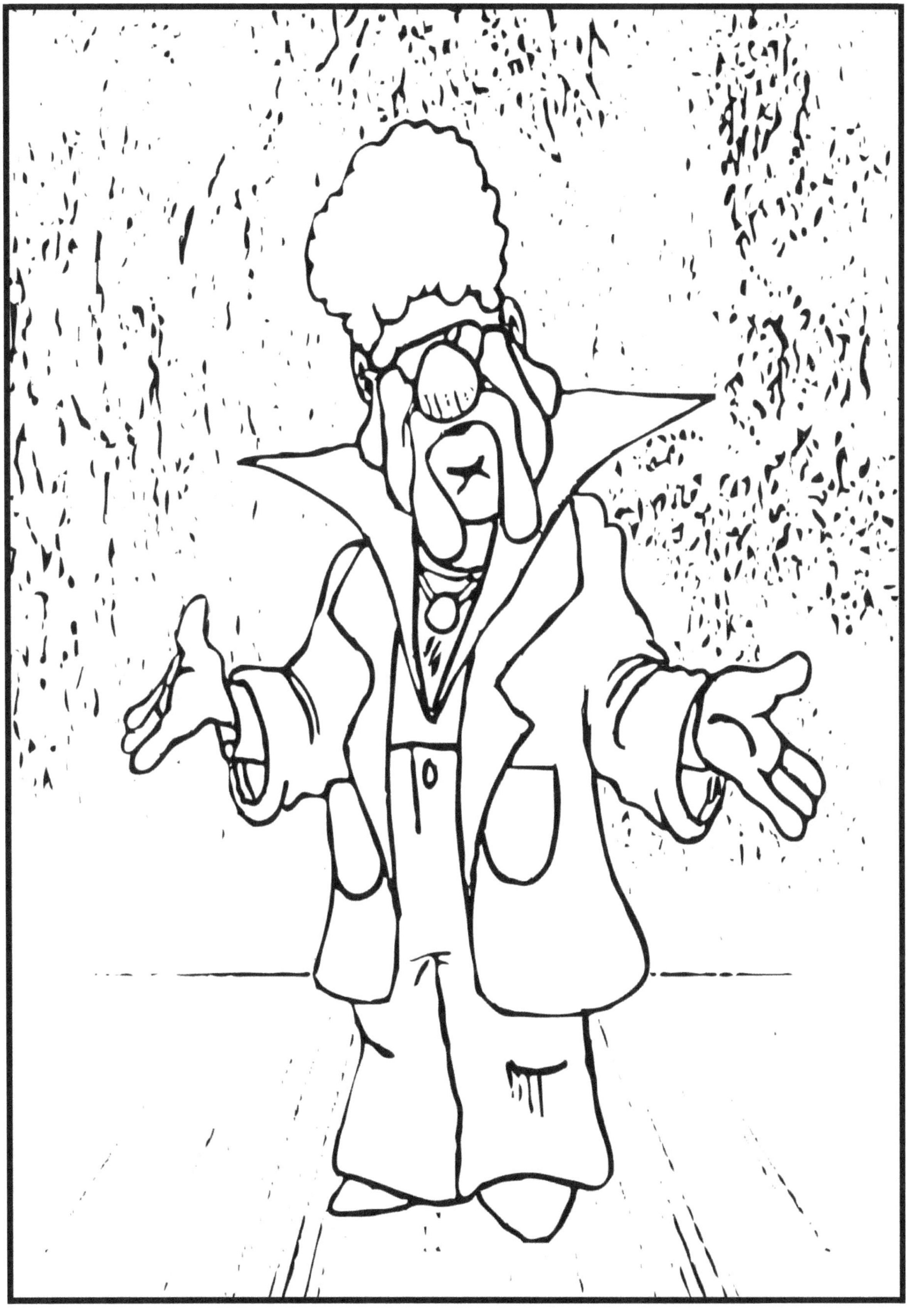

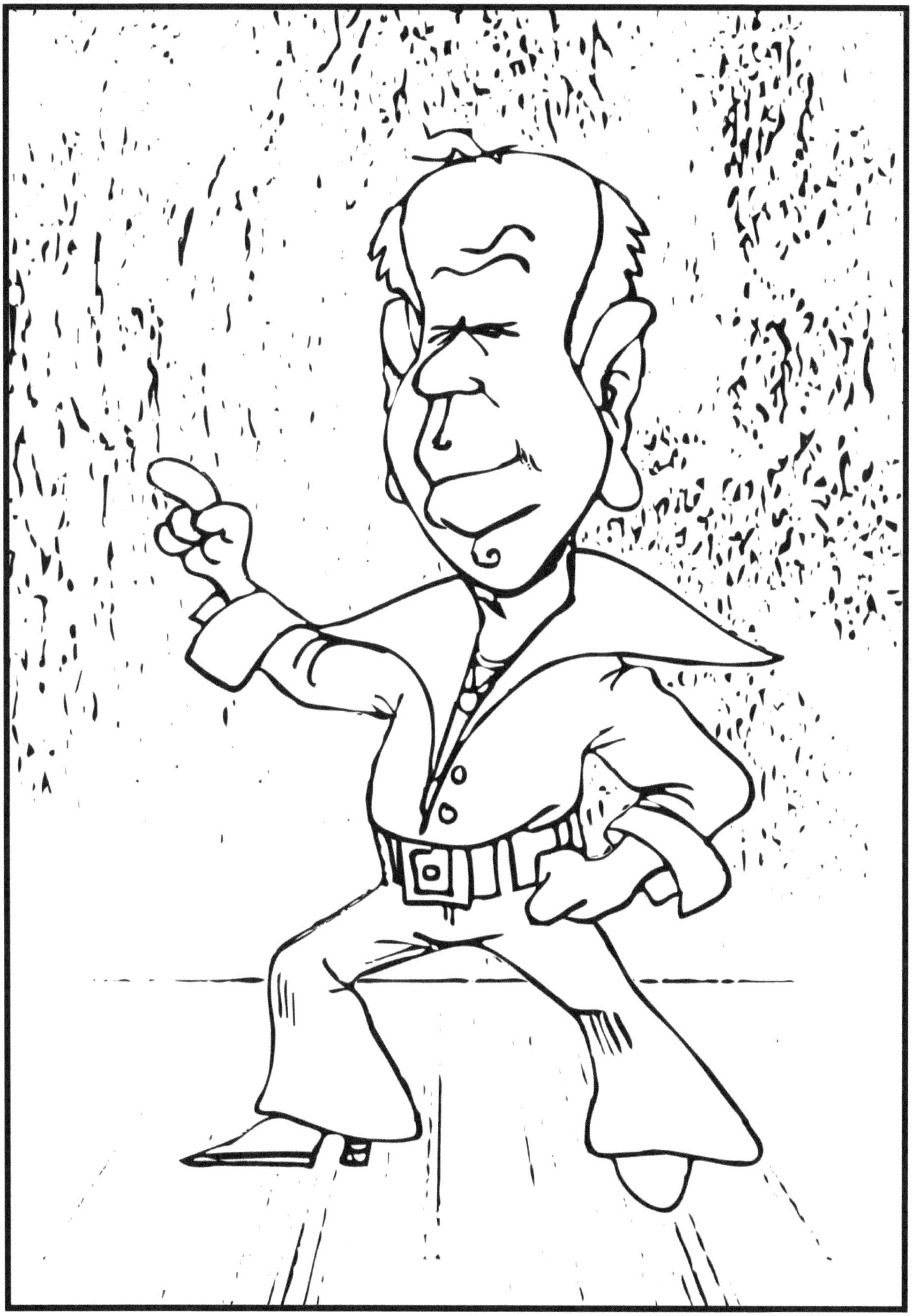

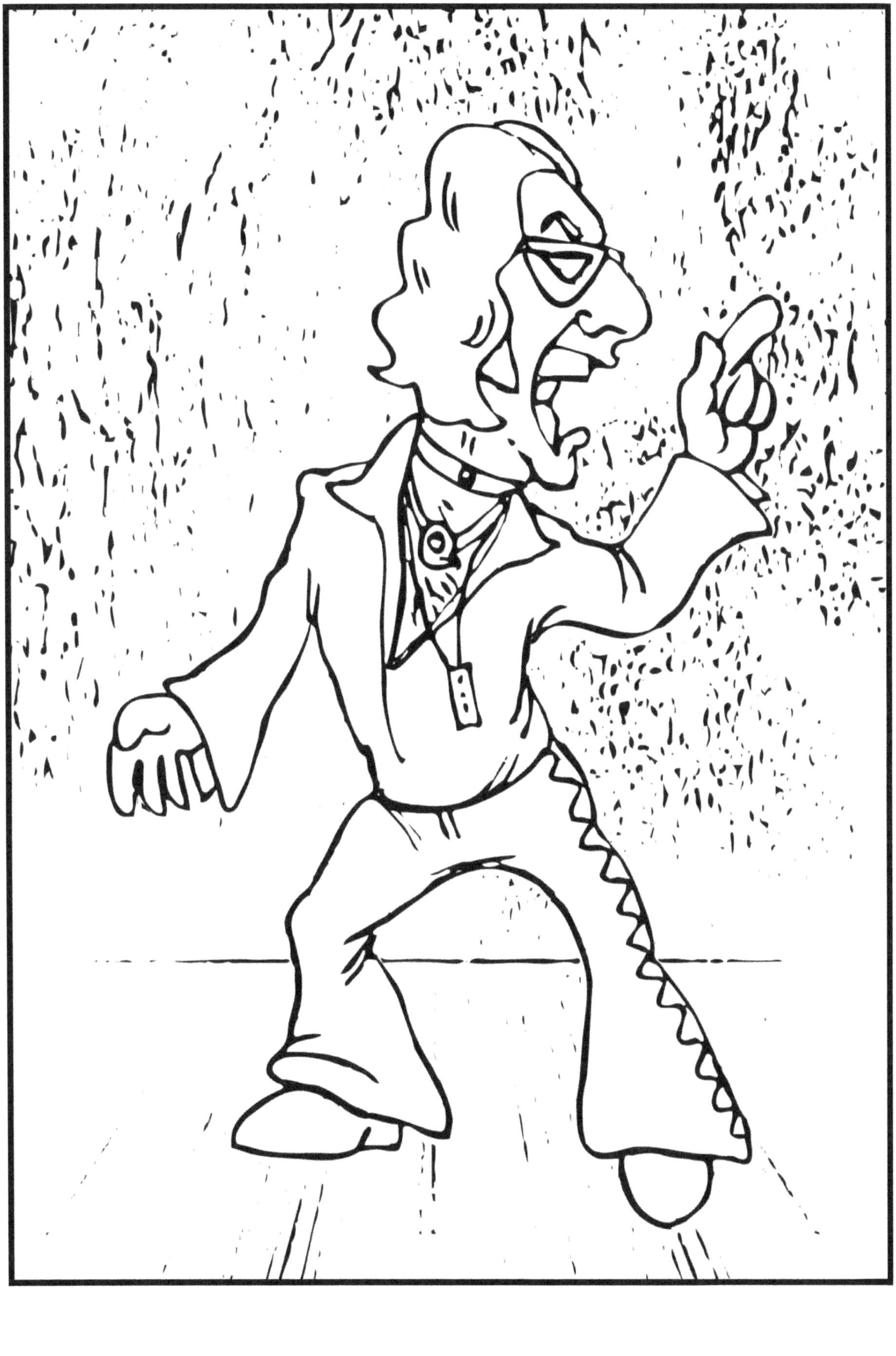

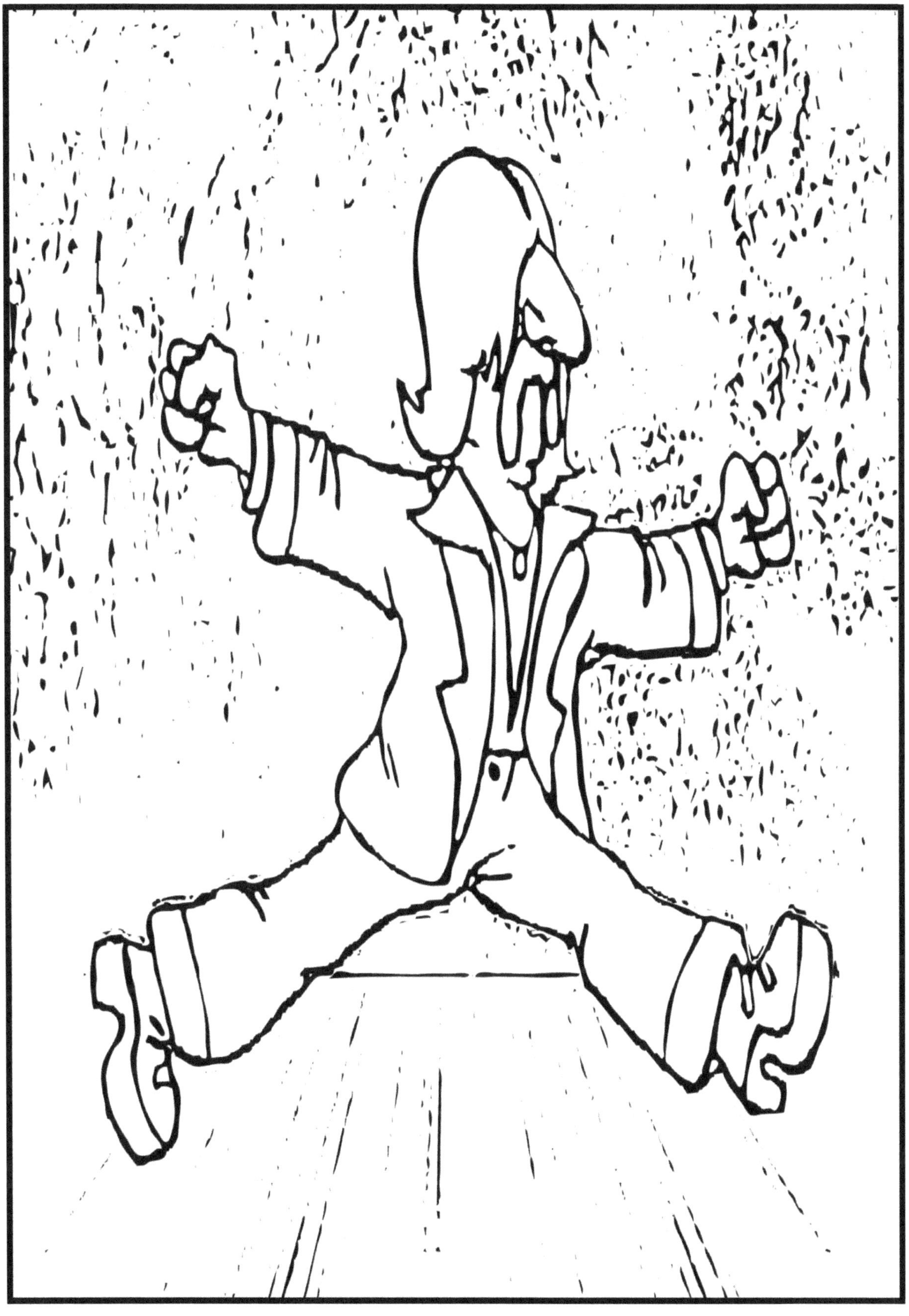

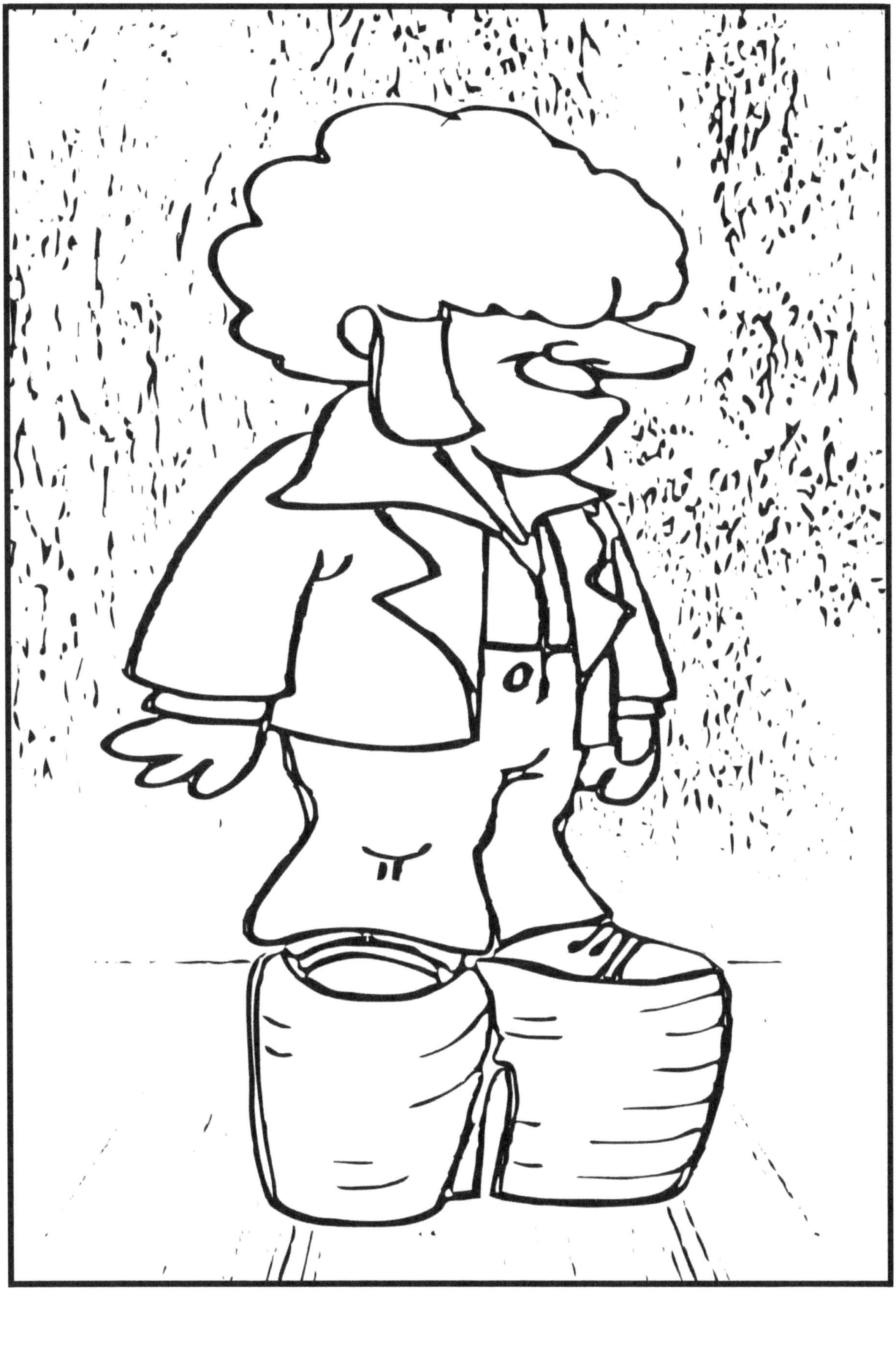

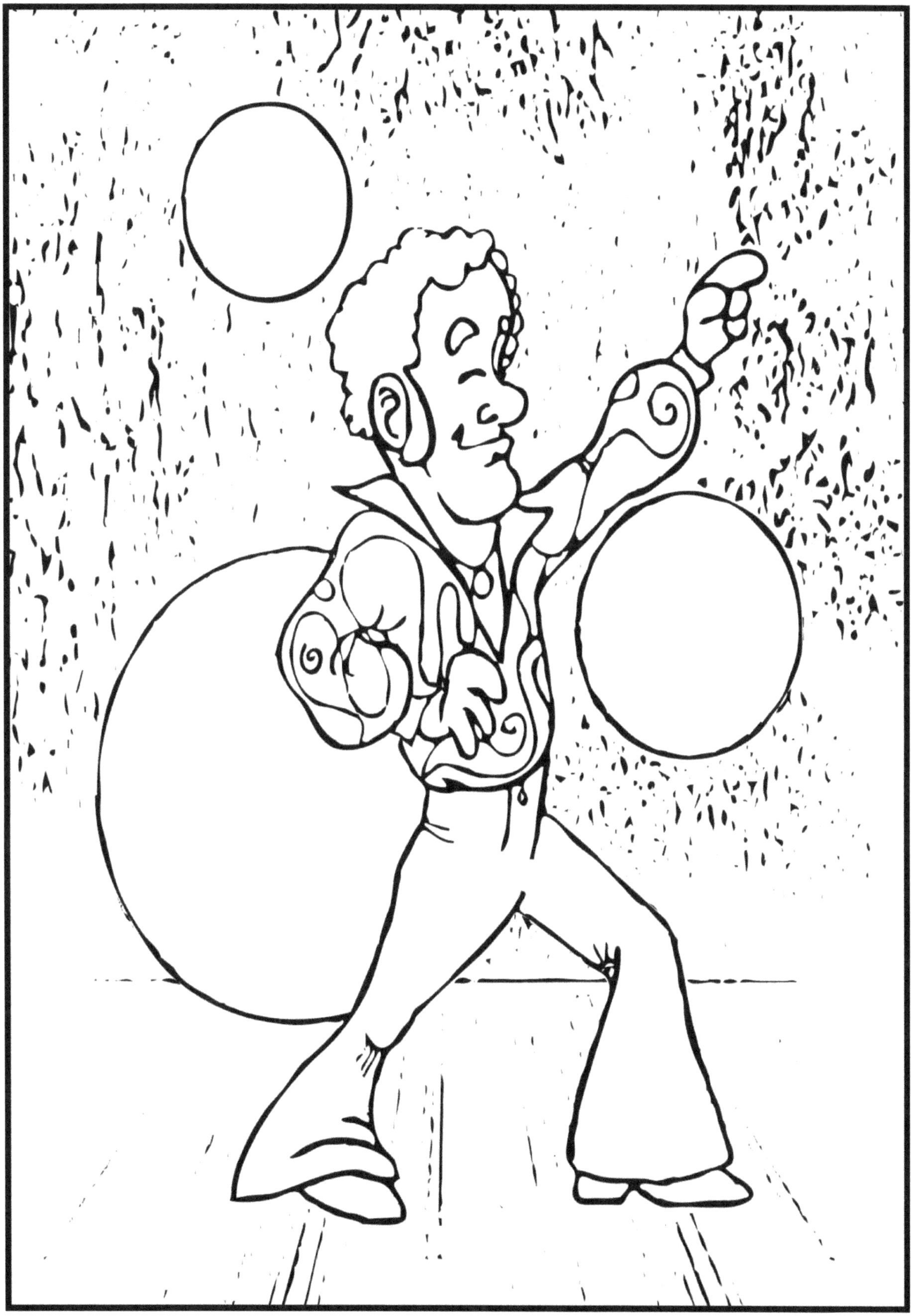

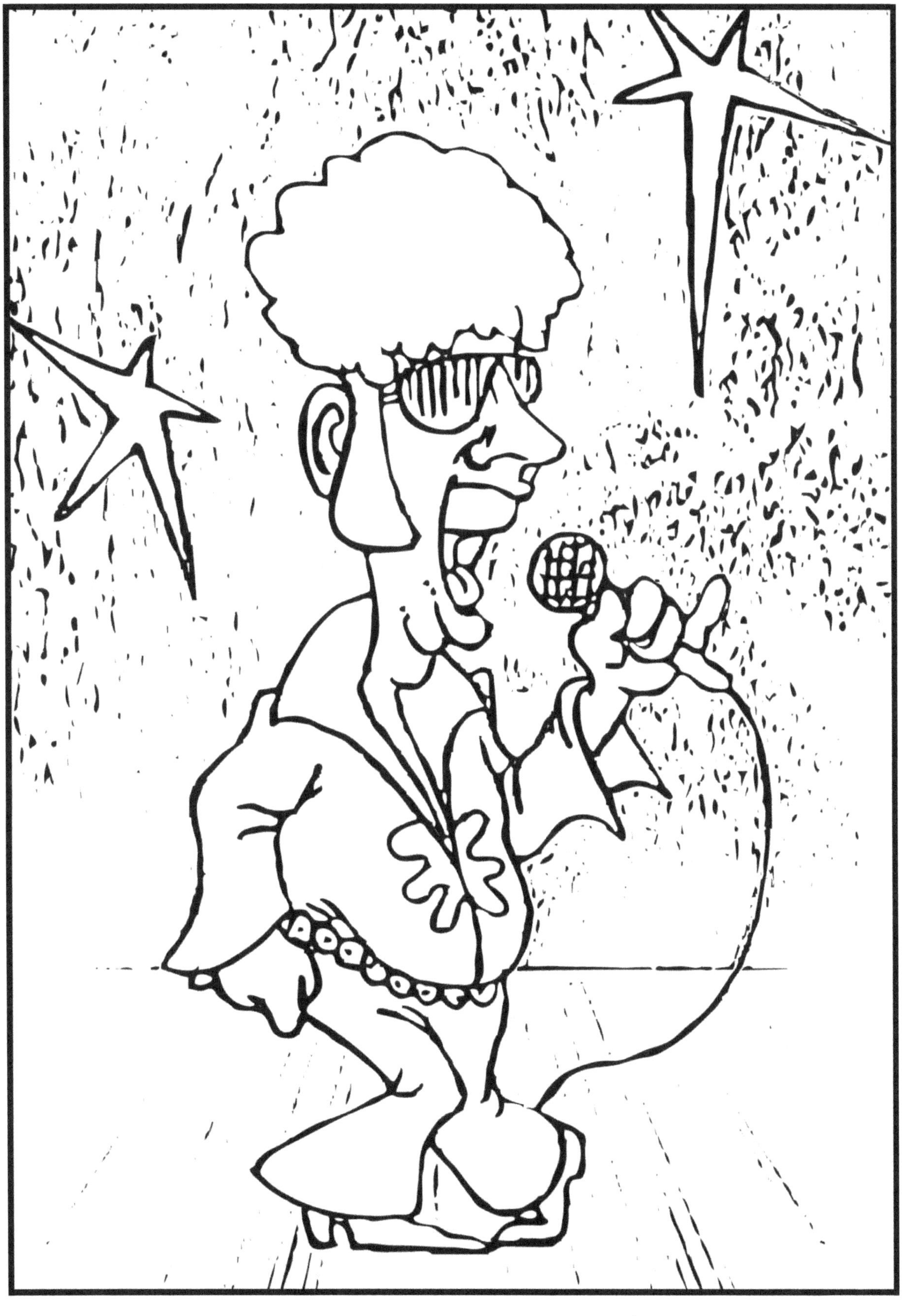

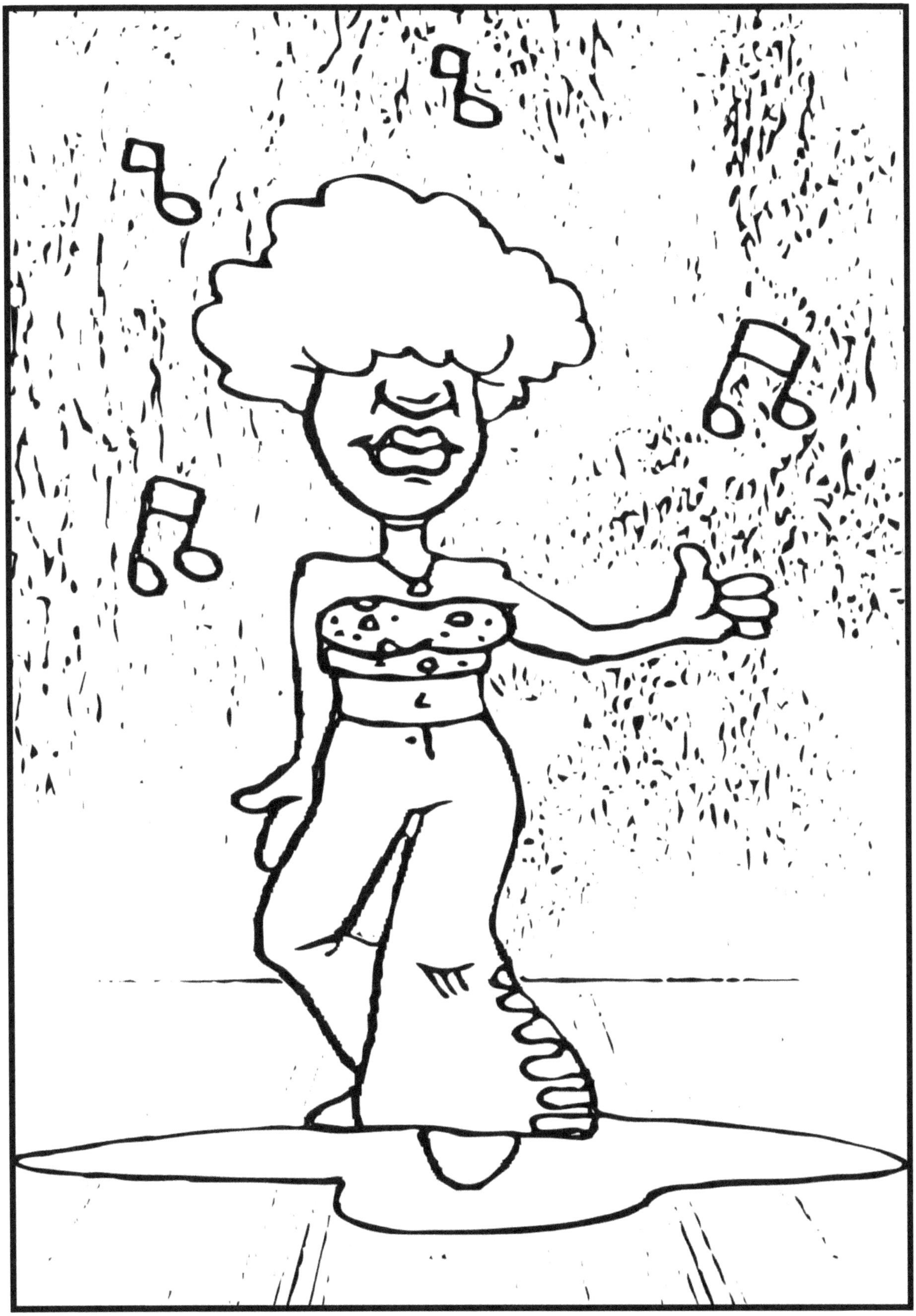

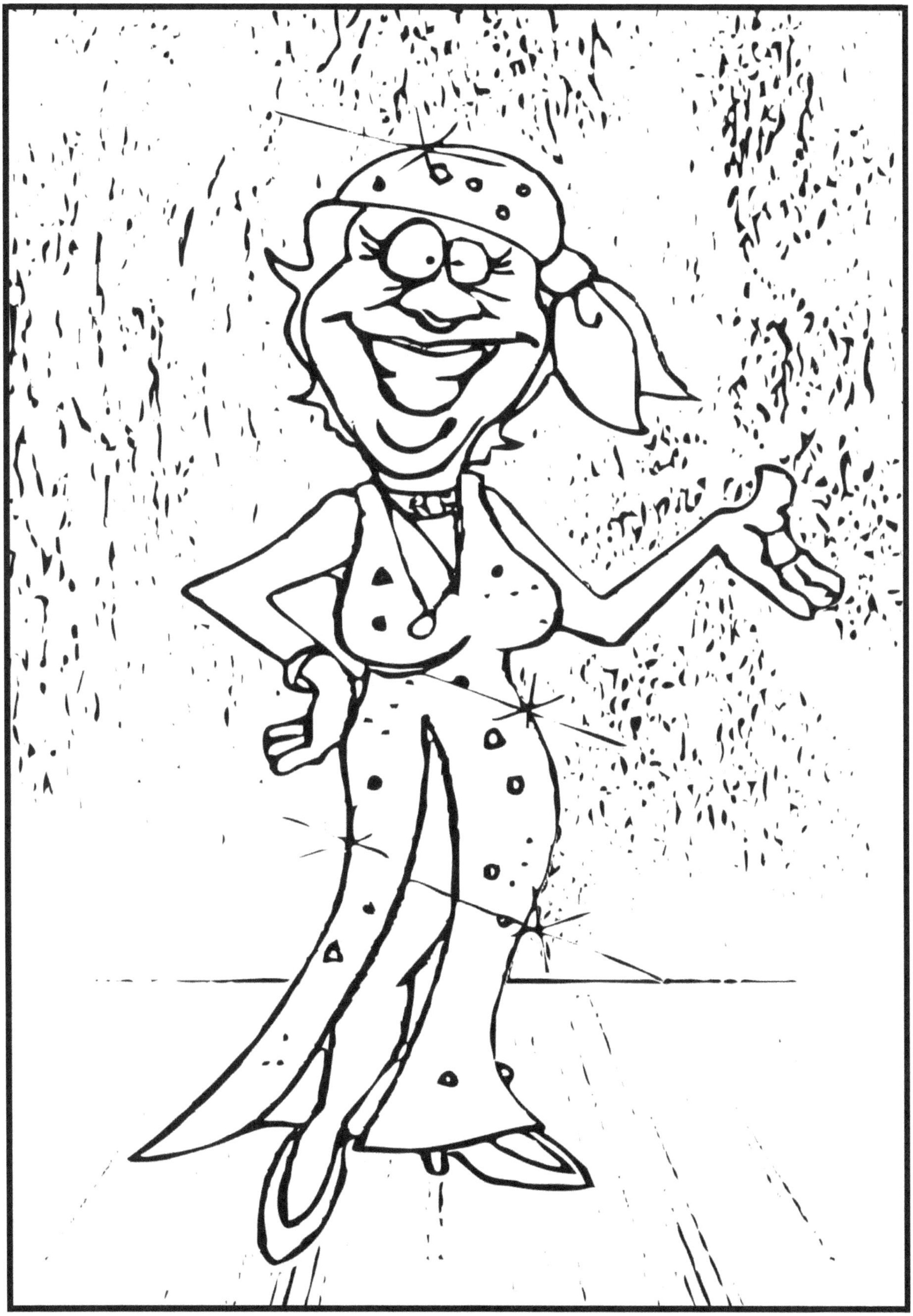

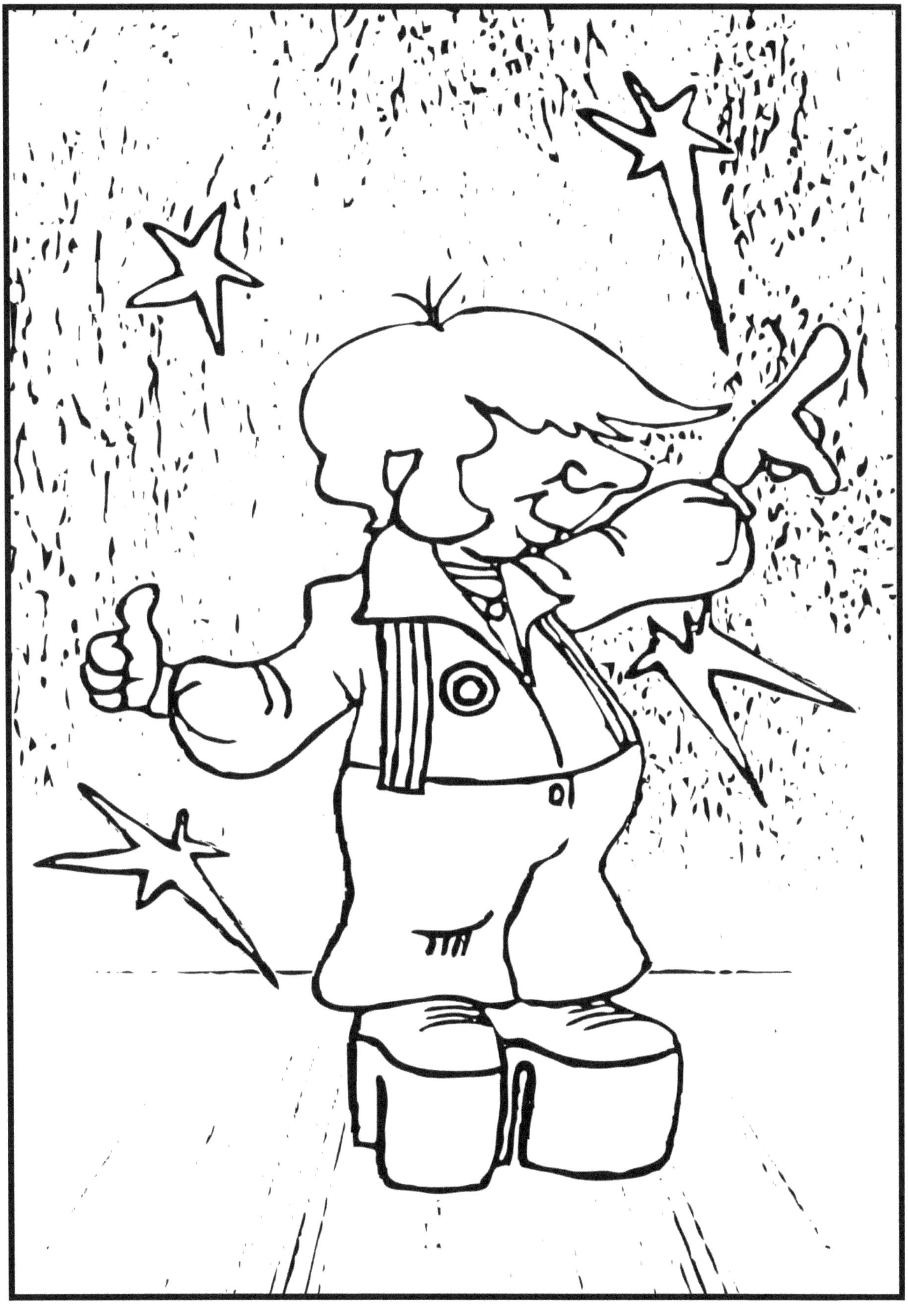

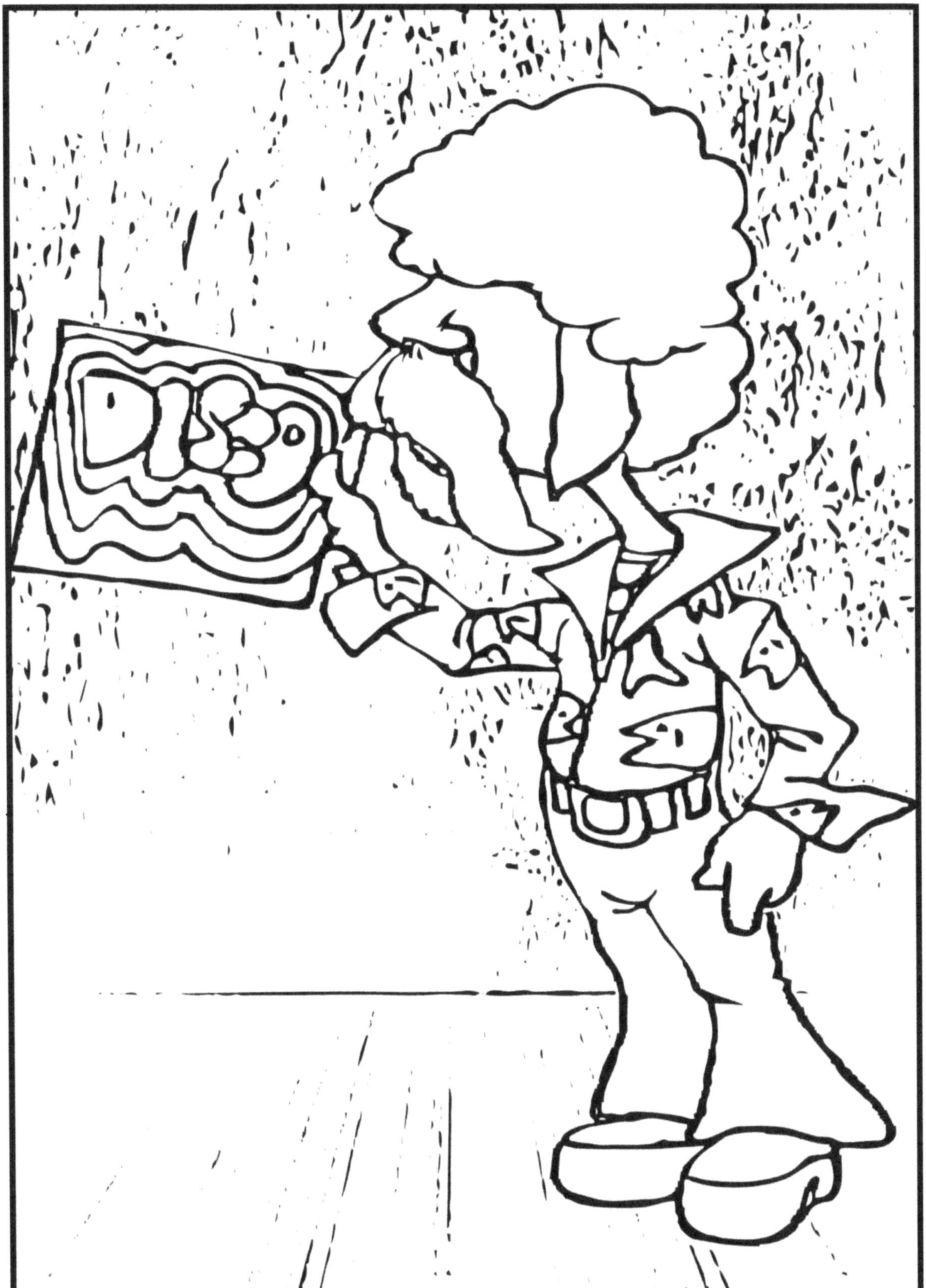

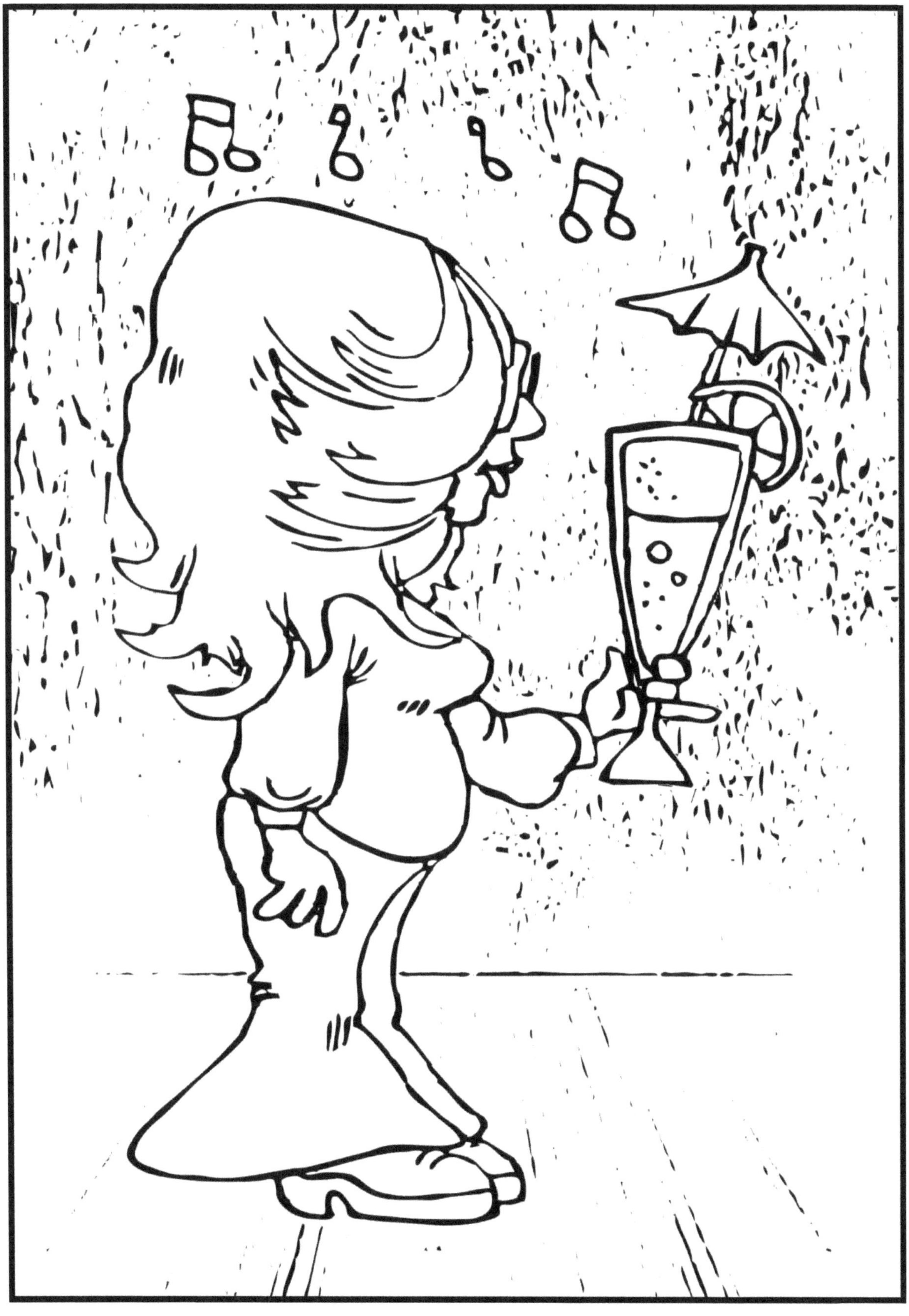

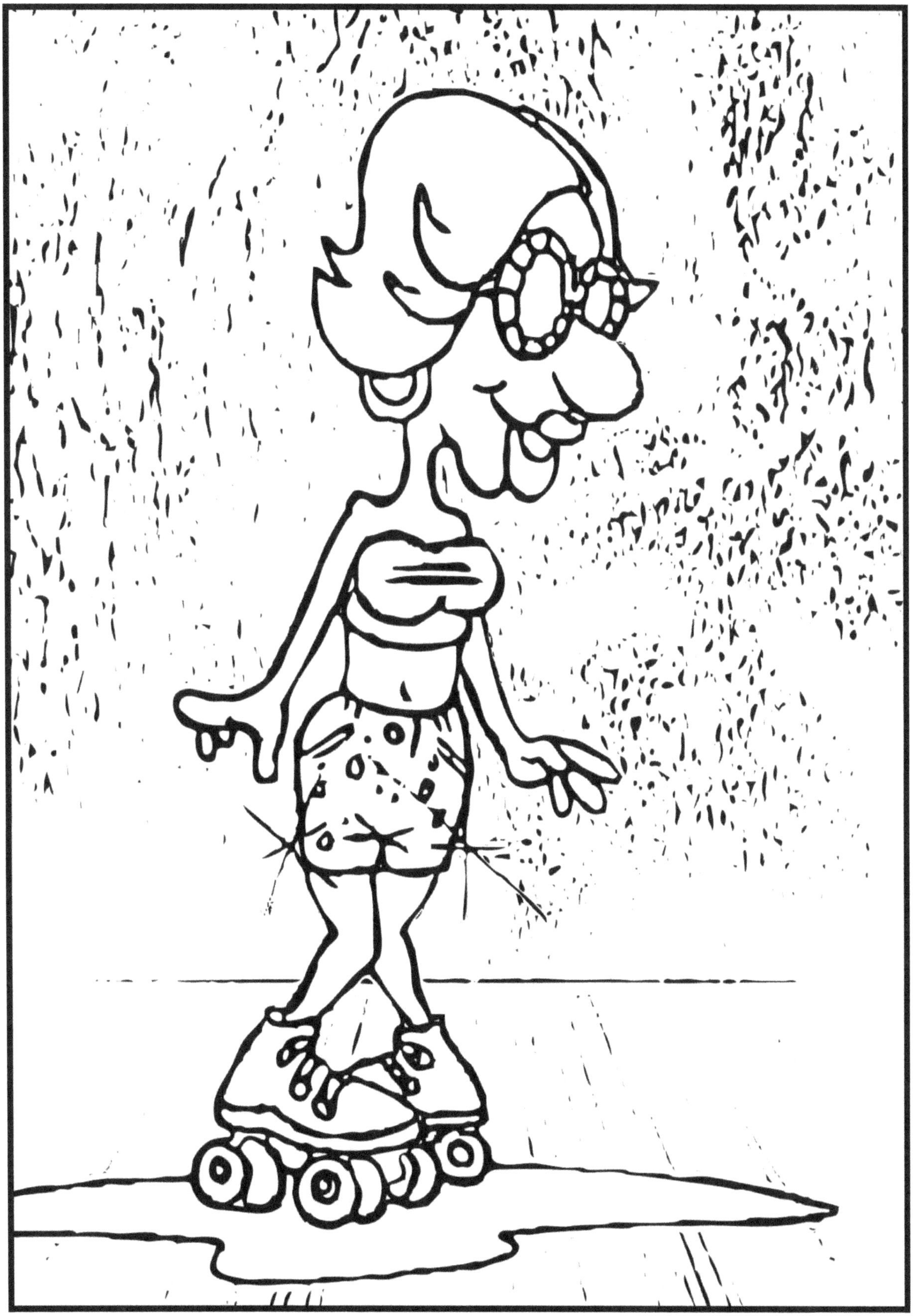

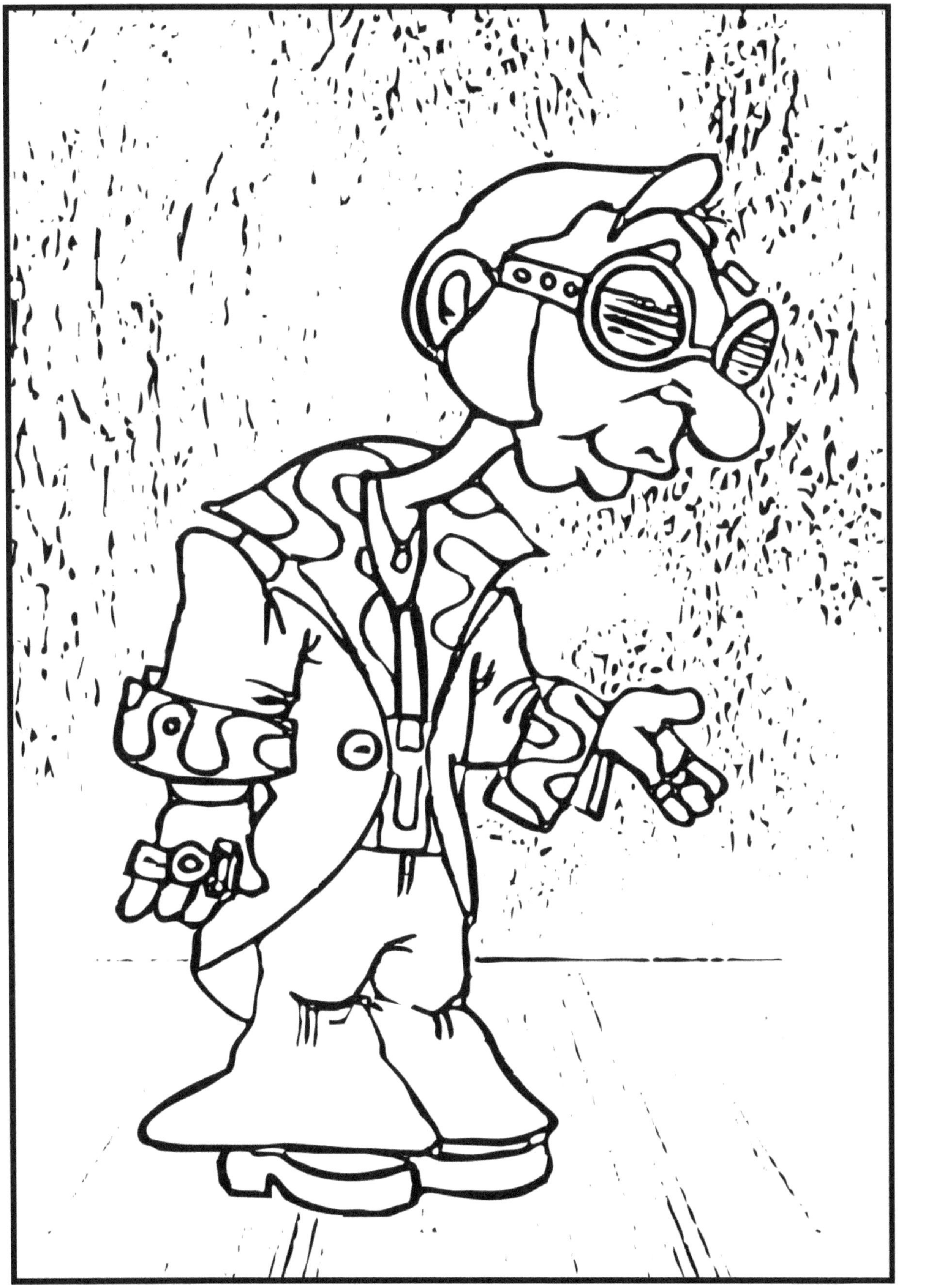

www.ingramcontent.com/pod-product-compliance
Lightning Source LLC
Chambersburg PA
CBHW081553170526
45166CB00009B/2680
9781522786832